Ian Black is Vicar of Peterborough and (Peterborough Cathedral. Prior to ordina He is married with two sons. He is the author oi *Calendar of Saints and Holy Days* and *Prayers for All Occasions*, also published by SPCK.

www.ianblack.org.uk

INTERCESSIONS

for Years A, B and C

IAN BLACK

First published in Great Britain in 2009

Society for Promoting Christian Knowledge
36 Causton Street
London SW1P 4ST
www.spckpublishing.co.uk

British Library Cataloguing-in-Publication Data
A catalogue record for this book is available from the British Library

ISBN 978–0–281–06021–4

Typeset by Graphicraft Limited, Hong Kong
First printed in Great Britain by Ashford Colour Press
Subsequently digitally printed in Great Britain

Produced on paper from sustainable forests

To the people of the parishes in
Maidstone, Davington, Oare and Whitkirk
and Canterbury and Ripon Cathedrals
where I have had the privilege of serving

Contents

———•◆•———

Contents

Contents

Introduction

————◆————

This book could be subtitled 'Praying with the Bible' because that is
what it invites you to do. Each set of intercessions is based on the Bible
readings set for the Sundays and Principal Holy Days of the Church's
year. These follow the three-year Revised Common Lectionary as
ordered for the Church of England. Each year is centred on one of the
first three Gospels (Year A – Matthew; Year B – Mark; Year C – Luke)
with John being used at key moments and to fill up certain spaces.
These prayers draw heavily on the Gospels, but also on the Old
Testament, Psalms and Epistle readings, especially where common
themes emerge. The Gospel provides the lens through which the other
readings are seen. I have tried to construct these in such a way that their
use is not dependent on all of the readings being used – I know they
aren't.

Most of these prayers were written in the thick of daily life. One set
was even written in Kwik Fit while waiting for a puncture to be
repaired, reminding us that prayer belongs in the midst of ordinary life,
not just in protected spaces. Through our prayers, God makes wherever
we stand holy ground.

Writing prayers and intercessions is more like writing prose than
narrative. What we look for are phrases, sometimes poetic in tone, that
excite prayer through opening up our offering to God and expanding
our imagination. We are not trying to dot every 'i' and cross every 't'.
So, whatever our words, they will be complemented by a generous
helping of silence in which to allow the Holy Spirit to move and extend
our praying.

In the main these prayers are compatible with the traditional pattern
of praying for the Church, political governance and world concerns, the
neighbourhood and local community, those who are sick or in special
need and the deceased. Each petition includes a focusing bidding,

followed by some dots (. . .) to encourage those using them to include topical and specific intentions. There is then a gathering sentence to draw the praying together before a responsory is used. I have found that many intercessors have used my previous book, *Intercessions for the Calendar of Saints and Holy Days* (SPCK 2005), with imagination, borrowing phrases that focus and deepen the theology of their praying and adding to these their own words. My hope is that this book will provide a frame in which many will find confidence to include their own words. Praying in our own words personalizes the offering and roots it in a specific place. Equally, the prayers can be used straight if something short and focused is required.

A bidding and response is given for each set of intercessions either reflecting the season or seeking to complement the themes emerging from the readings. Many of these are taken from the Psalms, which provide a rich resource for such responses. These responses are optional, and in some settings familiar forms from the regular liturgy will be preferred. Equally a customary response can be combined with the bidding offered here, if that is easier to remember. The time of prayer needs to be introduced, but in no more than a sentence. It is after all the invitation to pray, not the prayer itself, and also not a mini sermon! 'Let us pray' is perfectly acceptable. Anything extra is embellishment. The intercessions will need to be concluded with a phrase that offers all of these prayers to God's grace and mercy. That sentence can be turned round into such a doxology: 'Trusting in your unfailing love, we commend these and all our prayers to your grace and mercy.' There is also provision in the supplementary pages of Common Worship, including the now classic phrase, 'Rejoicing in the fellowship of all your saints, we commend ourselves and the whole creation to your unfailing love.'

I am conscious that many intercessors seem to find it difficult to find words when praying for the Church; to find the way in to prayer. My aim has been to begin each set of intercessions with a petition that lifts our praises and focuses on our hopefulness in God. If nothing else, I hope these prayers will enrich the praying.

I am grateful to those who have provided the community in which many of these prayers have been 'road-tested'. This has primarily been at early morning Eucharists on Sundays. The places where I have served have provided the well from which I have drawn for their grounding and the book is dedicated to them with much love and gratitude. I hope others will find them an encouragement to pray and an aid to having our confidence in God's grace and mercy renewed.

Ian Black

Advent 1

Year A

Come, let us turn to the Lord
Let us call upon his name.

Lord, we watch and wait for your dawning Kingdom.
Teach us to walk in the way of your Son . . .
Gladden the hearts of your people.

Lord, we watch and wait for your reign of peace.
We pray for Jerusalem and the Middle East . . .
May all nations lay aside the ways of darkness and put on the armour of
    light.

Lord, we watch and wait in your saving presence.
Be in our communities, places of work and all centres of education and
    learning . . .
Draw us to seek the good of all.

Lord, be with all who watch and wait by the side of someone they love.
We pray for all who are alone, fearful and anxious . . .
May your Advent Hope sustain us through the dark hours.

Lord, we watch and wait for your coming in glory.
Preserve us at the hour of our death . . .
May your holy angels carry the faithful departed to your eternal home.

Year B

Tear open the heavens and come down, O Lord
Make known your name.

Lord Christ, we look to your coming again.
Come among us with mercy and judgement.
When you come may we be found prepared and ready to greet you
    with faith and hope . . .
Set the heart of your Church on your redeeming presence.

Lord Christ, we look to your coming again.
Come among the nations with mercy and judgement.
Keep those in government alert to your justice and peace . . .
Expand the vision of your people to that of your eternity.

Lord Christ, we look to your coming again.
Come among our communities and homes with mercy and judgement.
Mould us as a potter shapes clay . . .
We are the work of your hands and rejoice in your gift.

Lord Christ, we look to your coming again.
Come among all who are ill with mercy and judgement.
Give time to amend life and to be thankful for your love . . .
Strengthen and hold them in the palm of your hand.

Lord Christ, we look to your coming again.
Come among us at the hour of our death with mercy and judgement.
Gather your faithful ones to your eternal home . . .
Turn our tears into dancing.

Year C

Remember us in your love, O Lord
We put our trust in you.

Lord Jesus Christ, we look for signs of your dawning Kingdom.
Keep your Church expectant for the fulfilment of your promises . . .
Keep us alert and focused on the hope of your coming.

Lord Jesus Christ, we look for signs of your justice.
Raise up rulers and leaders of integrity and peace . . .
Give your people cause to sing the song of your freedom.

Lord Jesus Christ, we look for signs of your renewal.
Refresh the face of the earth, breathing new life into the fallow ground . . .
Sustain us with your abundant grace.

Lord Jesus Christ, we look for signs of your righteousness.
Strengthen the hearts of all who are anxious or in distress . . .
Remember us, O Lord, in your compassion and love.

Lord Jesus Christ, we look for signs of your redemption.
Restore to life all who have died in faith or fear . . .
You are our salvation and we trust in your mercy.

Advent 2

Praise the Lord, all the earth
Let all people praise you.

Blessed Lord, you prepare a pathway to your presence and call us to
  repentance.
Give courage to your Church to announce your Kingdom . . .
May we be rooted and grafted into your Son.

Blessed Lord, you challenge the powerful and restore the weak.
Bring all nations to the ways of justice and peace . . .
By the power of your Holy Spirit, may we abound in hope.

Blessed Lord, you heal the divisions and hurts that drive a wedge
  between communities.
Bring us to live in harmony with one another . . .
Together, with one voice, we will glorify you.

Blessed Lord, you come to everyone in their need, and your compassion
  overflows to cover the earth.
Pour out your healing and life-giving presence on all for whom we
  pray . . .
May the whole earth be filled with your glory.

Blessed Lord, when our hearts are aching, you hear our cry.
Open the door of your Kingdom to all who have died . . .
Bring us to dwell in your courts for ever.

Year B

God is gracious
Your salvation is near.

Lord, you make a road through the wilderness and desolate places to
  meet us.
Turn our rebellious hearts to embrace the promise of your
  redemption . . .
Give grace to your Church to prepare your people in holiness and
  godliness for your coming among us.

Lord, our moments are held in your eternity and the glory we create is
  like the passing grass of the field.
Give to all leaders of nations wisdom and courage to face the longer
  vision . . .
Bring in your justice now and for the future.

Lord, you honour your creation by your presence.
We give you thanks for all with whom we share life's joys and sorrows,
  rest and labour . . .
Transform our relationships to reflect your love and respect.

Lord, in our strength and weakness your glory is made known.
Give patient hope to all who are ill or recovering from treatment . . .
Reach out with your healing touch.

Lord, comfort your people in their grief and distress with the promise of
  your saving love.
Gather to yourself all who have died . . .
Bring us to rejoice in your salvation.

Year C

Blessed be the Lord our God
Who guides our feet into the way of peace.

Saving God, you sent John to prepare the way for your Son.
Give your Church grace to hear the cry in the spiritual wilderness . . .
Transform our hearts to be open to your Spirit.

Saving God, you sent John to straighten the crooked and level the rocky
    path.
Challenge devious minds with your justice and truth . . .
Raise leaders of integrity and passion.

Saving God, you sent John to baptize for repentance and forgiveness.
Give to all people humility to examine their lives with honesty and
    devotion . . .
Turn us away from the deceit of self and others.

Saving God, you sent John empowered by your word.
Speak your words of healing to all in anguish or distress . . .
Bless us with your love and mercy.

Saving God, you sent John to announce your redeeming presence.
Receive into your tender care all who have died . . .
May we come to see your salvation.

Advent 3 – Gaudete Sunday

Year A

Rejoice, the Lord is near
Come, Lord Jesus.

Liberating God, we rejoice in your freedom and our hearts sing for joy
  in your salvation.
Open our lips to proclaim your Son . . .
Inspire your Church to delight in your presence.

Eternal Lord, you rule over the heavens and the earth.
Transform our politics that all may have cause to rejoice and celebrate
  the fulfilment of your promises . . .
Stir all nations to honour the dignity of all people.

God of justice, as we look to celebrate again the birth of your Son,
increase within us your compassion and mercy for all who are hungry,
  excluded or on the margins of our society . . .
May your promises be shown in deed as well as word.

God of healing and hope, be with all whose hands and limbs are swollen
  with arthritis or whose abilities are restricted.
We pray for all who are disabled in any way . . .
Refresh all who are dry and thirsty for relief in their sufferings.

Lord of life and love, in your Son you bring salvation.
Sustain children who mourn parents and all whose hearts grieve . . .
May the good news of your Son rising in glory fill our hearts with
  rejoicing.

Year B

Rejoice in the Lord
Give thanks to his holy name.

We rejoice, O Lord, in your liberation.
May your Church proclaim your freedom and release . . .
Set us free from all that holds us back from proclaiming your glory.

We rejoice, O Lord, in your justice.
Guide the nations in ways that enable all people to sing for joy . . .
Restore your balance in trade and cohesive living.

We rejoice, O Lord, in your favour.
Pour out your grace on our communities that they may abound in your
    love . . .
Bless our homes and those closest to us with whom we delight in your
    praise.

We rejoice, O Lord, without ceasing, giving thanks in all circumstances.
May we hold fast through whatever trials may beset us . . .
God of peace, sanctify and keep us in your faithfulness.

We rejoice, O Lord, in your eternal mercy.
Hold dear to yourself all who have passed from glory to glory . . .
Count us acceptable in your sight at your coming again.

Year C

Rejoice in the Lord always
Sing aloud to God.

Let us rejoice and give you thanks, O Lord, for you challenge and
    inspire your people.
Make your Church expectant with your promise . . .
As we rejoice in you, let your gentleness be known.

Let us rejoice and give you thanks, O Lord, for you demand equality
    and justice.
Move the hearts of all in positions of power to rely on truth above
    status . . .
As we rejoice in you, fill all people with your virtue and well-being.

Let us rejoice and give you thanks, O Lord, for you excite us with your
    presence.
Transform our greed with the generosity of your grace . . .
As we rejoice in you, turn us from hatred to love.

Let us rejoice and give you thanks, O Lord, for you pour out your
    compassion and mercy.
Be with all who cry out in distress and infirmity . . .
As we rejoice in you, so may we be filled with your healing Spirit.

Let us rejoice and give you thanks, O Lord, for you give life to the
    dead.
We commend to you all whom we remember in love . . .
As we rejoice in you, bring us to share in the joy of your eternity.

Advent 4

Year A

Restore us, O Lord
And we shall be saved.

God of grace, you bring salvation to birth in Mary's Child.
May your Church be expectant with hope and promise . . .
Send us out to proclaim your good news with joy.

God of grace, you surprise us with the gift of your presence.
Stir up your strength and be among all rulers and civic leaders . . .
Grant that all may flourish and delight in your peace.

God of grace, we pray for all who have life growing within them:
those who greet this news with longing and those fearful of what it
    might mean . . .
Bless all parents and those who support and care for the young.

God of grace, we pray for all who eat the bread of tears and long for
    relief in their sufferings . . .
Send your Holy Spirit to overshadow us with the promise of your
    salvation.

God of grace, you give life to all who trust in you.
Hear our prayer of thanksgiving for all who have died . . .
In times of darkness, may the light of your presence bring comfort and
    the hope of heaven.

Year B

Proclaim the greatness of the Lord
Rejoice in God our Saviour.

God Most High, you overshadow us with the power of your Holy
  Spirit.
Bring to birth the promise of your hope in lives of holiness and
  grace . . .
Give to your Church courage to be servants of your will.

God Most High, you set before leaders a vision of justice and peace.
Guide them in ordering the common good for the benefit of all . . .
Bring to light the signs of your dawning Kingdom.

God Most High, with you nothing is impossible.
Hear the cry of all whose hearts ache at being childless . . .
Bring to fruition our creative love and longing.

God Most High, your favour rests on the lowly and moves to bless our
  bodies.
Restore within our frailty the image of your love . . .
Give rest, refreshment and hope to all who seek your healing grace.

God Most High, you announce salvation in the midst of our mortality.
Remove our fear at the hour of our death . . .
We will rejoice and sing of your enduring love.

Year C

God of mercy
Holy is your name.

Gracious God, our hearts leap for joy at your presence.
Be with your Church as we prepare to celebrate again the festival of
    your birth . . .
Increase our faith to trust in the fulfilment of your word.

Gracious God, you upset the hierarchies of this world.
Open the hearts of local and national governments to ensure the hungry
    are fed and that due regard is given to all with equity . . .
Come, Prince of Peace, and reign.

Gracious God, you bless us in the company of friends.
Bless all who support new and expectant parents . . .
Bring to birth safely the fruit of your promise.

Gracious God, you hear our cries of delight and agony.
Reach out with haste to all who call upon you . . .
Stir up your strength and come to our aid.

Gracious God, you redeem your people.
Raise all who have died . . .
We will rejoice in you our Saviour.

Christmas

———◆———

Set I (Years A, B and C)

God of grace
We behold your glory.

Wonderful Counsellor, your glory burst through the heavens to amaze
   the shepherds with news of your birth.
Bring us to kneel in adoration and worship . . .
May your Church proclaim your salvation from day to day.

Mighty God, you judge with equity and your power stoops to touch our
   humanity.
Inspire the rulers of the nations with this humility and concern for
   everyone . . .
Bring harmony and dignity to all peoples.

Everlasting Father, your name is exulted in all generations.
Bring the sounds of rejoicing and laughter to our homes . . .
Wrap your children in tenderness and love.

Prince of Peace, in your freedom we thrive and flourish.
Be with all whose hearts are troubled or distressed . . .
Bless us with your godly hope.

To us a child is born and he brings redemption for all who trust in him.
Hear our prayer for all who rest in your peace . . .
May your light dawn upon us with joy.

Set II (Years A, B and C)

God of grace
We behold your glory.

God of glory, with the shepherds we kneel in adoration
before the wonder of your saving love in Christ Jesus . . .
May we too leave rejoicing at your amazing grace.

With Joseph and Mary we journey to the city of the shepherd king.
Bind us together as one human family . . .
May your redemption touch all with justice and peace.

Light of the world, you made your bed in a borrowed manger.
Be with all who are in strange places *tonight/today* . . .
Guard and keep all refugees and displaced peoples.

Christ the Lord, your loving-kindness brings joy and gladness to the
    frightened and anxious.
Hold in your tender gaze all who are troubled in any way . . .
May the good news of your birth fill us with your light and truth.

Lord, the heavens declare your righteousness.
Gather to yourself all who are treasured in your heart and whom we see
    no longer . . .
With the whole host of heaven, bring us as heirs to the hope of eternal
    life.

Set III (Years A, B and C)

God of grace
We behold your glory.

Eternal God, your Word brings everything into being, and in your grace
we are adopted as your children.
Teach us to honour and respect the imprint of your essence in all
people . . .
Your light shines in the darkness and nothing can overcome it.

Word of life, you inspire prophets to tell of your wonders and call your
people to walk in your ways.
Guide the steps of those who sit in government . . .
Bring justice and peace for the good of your whole creation.

Spirit of truth and wisdom, you bring hope to birth and lighten the
hearts of all who call on you.
May this celebration of our Saviour's birth renew within us the good
news of your gift . . .
Bless all with whom we exchange tokens of love and expand our
concern to embrace strangers and unknown friends.

Blessed Lord, shine your light on all who walk in darkness;
any for whom this season heightens distress . . .
Anoint them with the oil of gladness.

Lord, you make ruined places break into song and restore all that has
been lost.
Lift the heads of all who are weighed down with grief and give your
new life to those who have died . . .
With the whole host of heaven, we will sing your praises and exalt your
name.

Christmas 1

Year A

Glory to God in the highest
And peace to his people on earth.

Lord of grace, your love is steadfast and we are saved by your presence
    in your Son.
Give to your Church the gifts of grace to proclaim your liberty . . .
We will exalt your name.

Lord of the persecuted and oppressed,
we pray for all who seek refuge from violent and murderous regimes . . .
As Christ's brothers and sisters unite us in peace and justice.

Lord of all creation, as the stars and planets reflect your glory, make us
    wise stewards of the earth . . .
Renew and sustain all that makes for truly abundant living.

Lord of mercy, you have pity on all who cry to you in their distress.
Be with all in need of your healing presence . . .
Give peace and hope to troubled hearts.

Lord of life and love, hear the cry of those whose grief is inconsolable;
for parents weeping for their children . . .
Through your death you destroy our death and bring us to rise in
    glory.

Year B

Glory to God in the highest
And peace to his people on earth.

All creation sings your praises, O Lord.
As your children, heirs of your grace, we kneel in adoration before
    you . . .
Bless your Church as we seek to share all that we have received.

News of your birth amazed the people and startled rulers.
Keep us from abuses which fear can trigger . . .
Raise up prophetic voices to challenge and inspire righteousness and
    peace.

After eight days your Son was circumcised under the law.
Bless newborn children and their parents . . .
Give wisdom to all who inspire the young.

You hold our lives, O Lord, through all the changing scenes.
Be with those enduring suffering or anxiety . . .
Give to troubled hearts the light of your presence.

Father, we glorify your name for your salvation in your Son.
In this hope and trust we commend to you all who have died . . .
With our whole being we will rejoice in you.

Year C

Glory to God in the highest
And peace to his people on earth.

God our Father, you hold us all our days and we grow in your love.
Give grace to your Church to respond to all enquiries with charity and
  patience . . .
May the word of Christ dwell in our hearts richly.

God our Father, bring in your reign of peace.
Bind together the disparate peoples of the earth in perfect harmony . . .
Bring all nations to rejoice together in your favour.

God our Father, at the turning of the year strengthen our resolve to
  walk in your righteousness.
We place in your service all that we have and are . . .
Put us to what you will, to your honour and glory with thanksgiving in
  our hearts.

God our Father, clothe us with compassion and kindness.
Hear our prayer for all in hospital or hospice . . .
Fill them with the joy of your presence.

God our Father, you are our beginning and our end.
In this faith and trust we commend to you our dearly departed . . .
Raise us with them to the place where there are no tears but one eternal
  praise.

Christmas 2

Years A, B and C

Glory to God in the highest
And peace to his people on earth.

God of grace and truth, your eternal Word brought life to birth and
    brings us to new birth in Christ Jesus.
Give strength and courage to your Church to testify to your saving
    presence . . .
Send us to be witnesses to your light.

God of grace and truth, inspire with justice and mercy all to whom is
    given the responsibility of government . . .
Guide all nations in the ways of peace.

God of grace and truth, illumine our hearts to resolve to follow you
    more clearly in this new year . . .
Forgive the sins of past mistakes and wilful neglect.
Bring to fruition the purposes of your love.

God of grace and truth, hear our prayer for all who are in hospital or
    hospice, and for all who keep vigil by their side . . .
Fill our hearts with the songs of gladness.

God of grace and truth, comfort all who mourn and bring to your
    eternal city those who have died . . .
Turn our sorrow into dancing and our mourning into joy.

Epiphany of the Lord
(6 January)

Years A, B and C

Lord, arise and shine
Make known your glory.

God of wonder and of light, by the guiding of a star the wise men came
  to worship your Son.
May your Church be a beacon to draw all people to kneel at your
  presence . . .
Give grace to all who share your name to proclaim your praise.

God of power and might, news of your Christ-child's birth filled Herod
  with fear.
Transform the hearts of all in political office to serve your Kingdom
  with joy . . .
With the offering of gold we place before you all our power and
  aspiration.

God of mystery and wisdom, in your Son you make known the purpose
  of your love.
Bless our homes and those with whom we share joy and laughter, pains
  and sorrows . . .
United in a common humanity, may we come to share the promises of
  Christ.

God of healing and restoration,
with myrrh we seek your anointing presence on all who suffer . . .
May our hearts thrill and rejoice in you.

God of glory, your radiance fills the heavens and our prayers rise to you
   like incense.
Hear us as we lay before you those who have died in faith and fear . . .
May we all come to see the dawning light of your rising glory.

Baptism of Christ
(Epiphany 1)

Year A

Lord, arise and shine
Make known your glory.

Spirit of God, descending like a dove,
anoint your Church with your life-giving and affirming presence . . .
Lead the people of your New Covenant to proclaim your glory.

Lord Jesus Christ, at your baptism you humbled yourself in preparation
  for service.
Anoint those who rule and govern with courage to uphold justice and
  goodly living . . .
Lighten the nations in the paths of righteousness.

God our Father, you make no distinction between peoples and invite all
  to come to you.
Keep us faithful to our baptism into your household of faith . . .
Guide our steps to delight in all you have made.

Holy and Blessed Trinity, you bind up our wounds, make us whole and
  restore us in your sight.
Pour your blessing upon all in sorrow, need or adversity . . .
Anoint and cheer our face with your abundant grace.

Lord, your people crossed the Jordan to enter the land of your promise.
In baptism death brings life.
Hear our prayer for all who have died . . .
Fulfil in them the hope eternal.

Year B

Ascribe to the Lord glory and strength
Worship the Lord in the beauty of holiness.

At his baptism your voice, O Lord, announced your beloved Son.
May all who are baptized in his name proclaim him in word and
deed . . .
Unite your Church in the waters of new birth by your Holy Spirit.

At the beginning of creation your Word, O Lord, brought everything
into being.
Give to your people reverence for all you have made that bears your
image . . .
May we be to one another a blessing.

In baptizing all who came, John displayed the hospitality of your love.
Increase within us the same spirit of welcome and openness to
repentance . . .
Unlock the chains of past mistakes and reveal the gateway to newness of
life for all.

At your command your Word, O Lord, brings light into darkness.
Shine your radiant beams on all who are in need of your healing
grace . . .
Bring us all to rejoice in your glory.

Your Word, O Lord, is our beginning and our end.
Into your loving purpose we commend all who have died . . .
May we at the last pass through the waters of death to live with you for
ever.

Year C

The Lord is with us
The Holy One is our Saviour.

In the wilderness and wild places, O Lord, you call your Church to
    proclaim your mercy.
Send witnesses to your glory to baptize in your name . . .
Pour out your Holy Spirit upon all who trust in you.

In corridors of power, O Lord, you call leaders to affirm your peace.
Raise up men and women to defend justice . . .
Give wisdom to all who shape laws and protect the vulnerable.

By the riverside and flowing streams, O Lord, you call people to repent
    and seek refreshment.
Renew our lives from all that dries up faith and damages trust . . .
Give hope to the cynical and despairing.

In sickness and in health, O Lord, you call us to sing your praise.
Lift up the hearts of all weighed down in pain and distress . . .
Give your people the blessing of peace.

In the hour of our death, O Lord, you call us to the place you have
    prepared for us.
Take away our fear through confidence in your redemption . . .
May we know that we are yours and held in your love.

Epiphany 2*

Year A

Lord, arise and shine
Make known your glory.

Faithful God, we give you thanks for your sanctifying presence in your
  Son.
Bless your saints throughout the world; everyone who calls on your
  name . . .
Put a new song on the lips of all who wait on you.

Jesus, Lamb of God, illumine the hearts and lives of all who seek your
  will.
We pray for those who express their faith in politics and strive for the
  common good . . .
Open the eyes of rulers and governments to seek your justice.

Lord, your call touches life before the cradle and beyond the grave.
Be with those who are expectant and hopeful as life emerges and
  develops . . .
In your sight all are honoured and given dignity.

Holy God, we seek your healing and life-giving Spirit.
In the circle of your love we hold all in special need . . .
Lift the despairing from the pit and set them on firm ground to trust in
  you.

Lord, your salvation reaches to the ends of the earth.
Hear us as we remember with thanksgiving those whose earthly labours
    are complete . . .
Restore us all in your grace and peace.

* *If the Feast of the Epiphany falls on a Sunday the readings set for Epiphany
    2 are actually used on the Sunday called Epiphany 3. A similar adjustment
    needs to be made on the following Sundays of Epiphany.*

Year B*

Ascribe to the Lord glory and strength
Worship the Lord in the beauty of holiness.

Lord, your call to Philip inspired him to encourage others to explore the
    wonder he beheld.
As your Church seeks to follow you so may we invite all people to
    'come and see' your glory . . .
Grant us a vision of your living presence.

Lord, Philip challenged Nathaniel's prejudice and disdain.
Overturn the ways we demean the value of others because of
    background, race or gender . . .
Open our hearts to discover your image in unexpected places.

Lord, friends shared discoveries of your Kingdom.
Bless those in whose company we can delight and flourish . . .
Restore in us the joy of life.

Lord, you saw Nathaniel from a distance.
Be with all who feel isolated or removed from their normal surroundings
    by infirmity . . .
Sustain us with your love.

Lord, you are always ready to greet us and call us home.
Draw to yourself all whose earthly life is over . . .
Bring us to delight in your eternity.

* *If the Feast of the Epiphany falls on a Sunday the readings set for Epiphany
2 are used on the Sunday called Epiphany 3. A similar adjustment needs to
be made on the following Sundays of Epiphany.*

Year C*

With you, O Lord, is the well of life
In your light we see light.

Lord Jesus, you fulfil our desires beyond our imagining.
Transform our failures and disappointments into new opportunities for
    your Kingdom . . .
Revive your Church in its mission to declare your love.

Lord Jesus, when provisions are low you open up a new generosity.
Teach us to share of our riches and poverty . . .
Give to leaders of nations renewed vision.

Lord Jesus, you shared in the joy of a wedding.
Bless all who are married and those preparing for marriage . . .
May each find in the other strength, companionship and delight.

Lord Jesus, you responded to need wherever you found it.
Bring your transforming love to bear on all who feel exhausted or
    drained in their suffering . . .
May we taste and see your goodness.

Lord Jesus, on the third day you rose for our salvation.
Gather to yourself all who have died . . .
Bring us to share with them in the wedding banquet of your Kingdom.

* *If the Feast of the Epiphany falls on a Sunday the readings set for Epiphany 2 are used on the Sunday called Epiphany 3. A similar adjustment needs to be made on the following Sundays of Epiphany.*

Epiphany 3

Year A

Lord, arise and shine
Make known your glory.

Christ our light, by the seashore you called Peter, Andrew, James and
John to follow you.
Unite your Church in common purpose to proclaim your Kingdom . . .
We will sing and make music to your glory.

Lord, you break the rods of oppression and set your people free.
Inspire with your justice all who lead and govern . . .
May your light shine in all lands of deep darkness.

Heavenly Father, we praise and thank you for our daily food.
Be with all mariners and those who harvest the seas . . .
Pour your abundant goodness on all our labours.

God our strength, your power to save is displayed in the cross of Christ.
Raise all who are in anguish or whose burdens are hard to bear . . .
Set them high upon your sure rock.

Lord, your light dawns on all who dwell in the shadow of death.
Hear our prayer for all who grieve and those who have died . . .
Do not forsake us, O God of our salvation.

Year B

Ascribe to the Lord glory and strength
Worship the Lord in the beauty of holiness.

God Most High, your glory continues to surprise our expectations
beyond our imagining.
Breathe new life into our traditions and familiar practices, to prepare
your people for your Kingdom . . .
Bless and guide your bride, the Church, as it seeks to live your good
news.

God Most High, you are with us in times of struggle and peace.
Strengthen the hand of those who defend the weak and vulnerable . . .
Give courage to those who dare to establish a just peace.

God Most High, you bring people together in love and fidelity.
Bless all who covenant their relationships before you . . .
In all that we are and all that we have we share in your love.

God Most High, you take our anxiety and rescue us from the pit of
despondency.
Give hope to all weighed down by concerns and fear . . .
Bring to troubled hearts the light and refreshment of your peace.

God Most High, we join our voices with the great multitude who cry
'Alleluia'.
In this faith and trust we bring before your throne of grace all who have
died . . .
May we come to share in the eternal banquet of your love.

Year C

With you, O Lord, is the well of life
In your light we see light.

Spirit of God, come upon your Church.
Fill it with your life and grace . . .
May we be good news to the poor in spirit and wealth.

Spirit of God, come upon the nations.
Challenge them with your justice and equity . . .
May we work for the liberty of all.

Spirit of God, come upon all weighed down by oppression and violence.
Inspire all who work for fair working conditions and levels of pay . . .
May our trading be a source of blessing.

Spirit of God, come upon all who have to overcome disabilities of mind
   or body.
Send your healing presence upon all in need . . .
May earth and heaven resound with your praise.

Spirit of God, come upon all who grieve and mourn.
Proclaim your favour to all who have died . . .
May we with them come to the fulfilment of your promised
   redemption.

Epiphany 4

———◆·◆———

Year A

Lord, arise and shine
Make known your glory.

Lord of righteousness, you reveal your glory in signs and wonders every
 day.
Transform our vision to trust in the fulfilment of your promises . . .
Sanctify your people with your Holy Spirit.

Lord of justice, you call all leaders and rulers to account for their
 upholding of your statutes.
Transform our politics to defend the poor and weak, to decide without
 partiality or prejudice . . .
Christ, by your power and wisdom, guide all nations in the ways of
 peace.

Lord of love, you invite us to share in your life and creation.
Transform our loving that we may delight in your covenant of
 grace . . .
May we share in the abundance of your love.

Lord of hope and faithfulness,
we place before your loving-kindness all whose grasp on hope is failing . . .
Transform our weakness with your strength.

Lord, with you is the well of life.
Shine your light on all who have died or are nearing death . . .
Raise us we pray to your love which touches the heavens.

Year B

Ascribe to the Lord glory and strength
Worship the Lord in the beauty of holiness.

Jesus, Holy One of God, your teaching astounded those in the
synagogue.
Build up your Church through godly preachers and teachers of your
word . . .
Excite our hearts to declare your glory.

Jesus, Holy One of God, your authority awakened the people.
Raise up leaders of vision and justice . . .
Sustain all who carry the burden of government.

Jesus, Holy One of God, your fame spread throughout the region.
Draw our hearts to value integrity above image and to know our worth
lies in your love . . .
May we model our lives on you.

Jesus, Holy One of God, your healing sparked amazement.
Give peace to all disturbed by ailments of mind, body or spirit . . .
Pour out your compassionate love.

Jesus, Holy One of God, you bring life to all in the shadow of death.
Raise up all who have died . . .
Bring us to rejoice in your courts for ever.

Year C

With you, O Lord, is the well of life
In your light we see light.

God of love, Simeon and Anna waited with patience hoping for the
    fulfilment of your word.
Increase in your Church this confident longing . . .
Reveal the light of your glory.

God of love, Simeon spoke of your Son as a sign that will be
    opposed.
Preserve all in power from the arrogance that creates division and
    strife . . .
Shape us as agents of your peace and justice.

God of love, Mary and Joseph made the customary offering for their
    first-born.
Be with all new parents as they care for and nurture their children . . .
Bless all who give support with parenting.

God of love, Simeon spoke of the sword that would pierce Mary's soul.
Hear the cries of anguish and desperation that come from all who watch
    and wait by the side of loved ones in distress and serious illness . . .
We wait on your loving-kindness, O Lord.

God of love, Anna spoke to all who looked for redemption.
Hear our prayer for all who have died . . .
Shine into the darkness of death and grief your light of hope.

Presentation of Christ in the Temple*
(2 February, or the Sunday falling between 28 January and 3 February)

———◼◆◀◼———

Years A, B and C

Lord of hosts
We praise your holy name.

Lord, your faithful servants Simeon and Anna watched in hope for the
  fulfilment of your promises.
Give to the Church the same patience and trust . . .
Give voice to your people to praise and speak of your redemption.

Lord, Simeon described your Christ as a sign that will be opposed.
Open the hearts of the powerful and those who are led to your
  justice . . .
Restore us in your peace.

Lord, you see our inner thoughts and we can keep no secrets from you.
Cleanse and revive our spirits for your praise and glory . . .
As we stand on holy ground, preserve us in truth and godly living.

Lord, we stand before you utterly dependent on your grace for all that
  sustains our living.
Teach us to praise you in sickness and in health . . .
Bring reassurance that though mortal we are precious in your sight.

Lord, you give leave to your faithful ones to depart in your peace.
Hear our prayer for all who have died . . .
May our eyes come to see your salvation.

* *See also Epiphany 4 (Year C) on page 34.*

Proper 1
(Between 4 and 10 February,
if earlier than 2 before Lent)

Year A

God of power and wisdom
Give your people the blessing of peace.

Blessed Lord, you call your Church to be a shining witness to your love
and glory.
Fill our hearts with joy and gladness to live the good news we
proclaim . . .
Bring to fulfilment the hope of your Word.

Blessed Lord, you challenge the rulers of this world with justice and
compassion.
Bring release to the oppressed, shelter to the homeless and food to the
hungry . . .
Raise the sights of all governments to honour the dignity of all people.

Blessed Lord, you affirmed those with you on the hillside by calling
them the salt of the earth.
We pray for all whose labours go unnoticed but uphold our common
life . . .
Unite us in the household of your Son.

Blessed Lord, when we are weary give us strength,
when we falter urge us on,
when we stumble and fall lift us up . . .
Refresh and sustain us with your never-failing streams.

Blessed Lord, your light breaks forth like the dawn.
In your mercy receive to yourself those who have died . . .
Bring us to rejoice in your rising glory.

Year B

Sing and give thanks to the Lord
For all his wonderful works.

Lord Jesus, amidst clamour and great demands you searched out a
   deserted place to pray.
Give your Church wisdom to be still before you . . .
Refresh and reinvigorate us for your service.

Lord Jesus, before you princes and rulers are brought to naught.
Take our economic and political aspirations and shape them to your
   Kingdom . . .
Mould us in your image.

Lord Jesus, you responded to Simon's concern for his mother-in-law.
Bless and support all who care for the elderly and those in residential
   care . . .
Be with all young carers and those struggling to cope.

Lord Jesus, your healing touch reached out to all who sought you.
Pour out your compassion on all whose needs we bring before you . . .
Sustain us in your love and mercy.

Lord Jesus, nothing can separate us from your love.
Remember for good those we commend to you . . .
Bring them and all the departed to share in your blessing.

Year C

When we call you answer
Great is your glory.

Lord Jesus, you taught your people from the shallows of the lake.
Inspire teachers of your word today to present your good news in
    accessible ways . . .
May the gospel of truth once again capture the imagination of this
    nation.

Lord Jesus, you encouraged tired fishermen to put out again into deep
    waters, delighting them with a catch beyond measure.
Raise up leaders who will inspire nations to strive for justice . . .
Give persistence and courage where opposition to your peace seems
    overwhelming.

Lord Jesus, friends and partners struggled together to haul in the catch.
Give us grace to work for all that strengthens the bond of communal
    life . . .
Sustain all that fosters the common good.

Lord Jesus, you brought encouragement to the weary and fresh hope to
    the despondent.
Lift the hearts of all weighed down with sickness or anxiety . . .
With hearts and voice we will praise you.

Lord Jesus, you appeared to your disciples risen from the dead.
Fill us with this hope in grief and at the hour of our death . . .
Bring us to rejoice in your salvation.

Proper 2
(Between 11 and 17 February,
if earlier than 2 before Lent)

Year A

God of power and wisdom
Give your people the blessing of peace.

Lord, your Son took your commandments and deepened their
   understanding.
Transform our hearts to show our love for you by walking more fully
   in your ways . . .
May we choose your abundant life.

Lord, you call your people to be reconciled and refrain from hate-filled
   talk.
Bring healing to all places of conflict and division . . .
May your fire and water purge and renew the nations of the earth.

Lord, purify your people to look upon one another with respect and
   honour.
Forgive our debased and vulgar abuse of our brothers and sisters . . .
Restore us in your image and dignity.

Lord, the weight of broken relationships presses upon your people.
Break the chains that oppress, and bring in your liberation . . .
Set us free to praise your name.

Lord, you set before us the hope of life everlasting.
In this confidence we entrust to you those who have died . . .
Fulfil your promise of redemption.

Year B

Sing and give thanks to the Lord
For all his wonderful works.

If you choose, Lord Jesus, you can cleanse your Church from its
    squabbling divisions.
Open our hearts to your transforming love . . .
As you call diverse people round your table, so may we honour our
    fellow guests.

If you choose, Lord Jesus, you can cleanse the world from hatred and
    vice.
Open our hearts to your justice and peace . . .
As you create diverse races and cultures, so may we honour our brothers
    and sisters in humanity.

If you choose, Lord Jesus, you can cleanse our communities from
    prejudice and bitterness.
Open our hearts to your rainbow creativity . . .
As you celebrate diverse ways of being, so may we honour the gifts they
    bring.

If you choose, Lord Jesus, you can cleanse us in our illness and sickness.
Open our hearts to your wholeness and healing . . .
As you pour out your healing touch, so may we honour all in need of
    care.

If you choose, Lord Jesus, you can break the hold of death.
Open to all who have died the gateway to your eternity . . .
As you raise us to new life, so you honour the purpose of your love.

Year C

When we call you answer
Great is your glory.

Blessed Lord, your Kingdom reverses the fortunes of all who are
    weighed down.
Make your Church to be a place where good news is announced . . .
Shape us to be living witnesses of your resurrection life.

Blessed Lord, your Kingdom challenges the complacency of all whose
    comfort makes them indifferent.
Give to all who lead the nations compassion for the poor and needy . . .
Give us the will to strive for justice.

Blessed Lord, your Kingdom extends beyond the narrow confines of our
    vision.
Extend our borders to embrace the rich diversity of humanity . . .
Give us grace to display the hospitality of your generous love.

Blessed Lord, your Kingdom brings healing in its wings.
Set free all bound by addictions and torments of the mind . . .
Look with mercy on all who call upon your name.

Blessed Lord, your Kingdom is our hope and our salvation.
Restore to life all who have died in Christ . . .
We will rejoice in your eternity.

Proper 3
(Between 18 and 24 February,
if earlier than 2 before Lent)

Year A

God of power and wisdom
Give your people the blessing of peace.

Holy God, you make the places we encounter you sacred.
As we belong to your Christ, so may your Church build on his firm
    foundations . . .
Build us as living temples for your praise and glory.

Holy God, you challenge your people with a justice based on
    righteousness, not fear.
Give us courage to uphold the rights and worth of all . . .
Incline our hearts to your truth.

Holy God, everything comes from you and we delight in your generous
    mercy.
Give us grace to show forth our gratitude with those who are friendly
    and hostile . . .
Transform the world with your amazing grace.

Holy God, in trials and joys your love reaches out to us.
You never leave us or forsake us, even when we feel alone and in
    darkness . . .
Let your light shine with hope and strength.

Holy God, you hold us in life and in death.
Remember for good those whose earthly life is over . . .
In your righteousness preserve us and keep us.

Year B

Sing and give thanks to the Lord
For all his wonderful works.

Lord, amidst great pressure and demands for healing,
you taught generous love both in word and deed.
Give to your Church a right balance between social care and teaching
    your word . . .
Unite our proclamation of word and action for your glory.

Lord, you challenged accepted assumptions in pronouncing the
    forgiveness of sins.
Lift false barriers that restrict fair liberties and constrict the spirit . . .
Set us free to rejoice in your peace.

Lord, people flocked to your door.
Strengthen all wearied by coping with crowds and heavy demands on
    services . . .
Be with call-centre staff and all who have to be the face of large
    institutions.

Lord, determined friends made a hole in the roof to reach you.
In your compassion bless all who are desperate for your healing touch . . .
We will declare your praise.

Lord, you gather your people to you.
Receive with love all who have died . . .
Be merciful to us and raise us up at the last day.

Year C

When we call you answer
Great is your glory.

Merciful Father, you break the cycle of hatred and recriminations.
Set your Church as an instrument of your peace . . .
May we sow love, pardon and faith.

Merciful Father, you bring dignity to the abused and oppressed.
Give to governments and rulers strength to prevent the worst excesses of
    retribution . . .
Restore us all in your image that we may forgive as we know ourselves
    to be forgiven.

Merciful Father, your compassion leaves no one excluded.
Open our hearts to the needs of the hungry, the homeless and all
    without sufficient to sustain them this day . . .
Give dignity to all your people.

Merciful Father, you hear the cries of all in distress.
Pour out your healing love on all who seek you . . .
Bring light to our darkness and joy to all in sorrow.

Merciful Father, your love holds us in life and in death.
Remember for good all who have died . . .
Keep the faithful departed forever in your loving embrace.

2 before Lent

Year A

God of power and wisdom
Give your people the blessing of peace.

In the beginning, your creating will, O God, brought all that there is
   into being.
In your gift we find our purpose and hope . . .
We give you thanks and praise, for your mercy endures for ever.

In your scheme and shape the world moves from darkness to light,
   from night to day, and returns.
Give balance and proportion to our striving . . .
Teach us to be still and be thankful for your enduring mercy.

In creating humankind in your own image you call us to wise
   stewardship of the earth.
Forgive our short-sightedness and wanton destruction . . .
Bring us to our senses and to live in harmony with all you have
   made.

In anxiety and despair we worry about what tomorrow will bring.
Teach us to be hopeful as we await the freedom of your sons and
   daughters . . .
With eager longing we trust in your steadfast goodness.

In hope we are saved, and we wait in patient anticipation of the glory to
   be revealed.
In this expectant faith we entrust to you those who have died . . .
May we with them come to share in your redemption.

Year B

Sing and give thanks to the Lord
For all his wonderful works.

God of wisdom, you proceeded forth at creation bringing life to birth.
Breathe that same potency into your Church . . .
As children of your grace bring us to rejoice in you.

God of wisdom, you delight in humanity.
Equip us to share that generous blessing in justice and peace . . .
Inspire with your wisdom all who lead and govern.

God of wisdom, you have set the world in a universe of order and
    intricate balance.
Guide all engaged in the advancement of science and the ensuing ethical
    debates . . .
It is through you and for you that we have our being.

God of wisdom, your fullness chose to dwell among us.
Give strength to all who are weak or whose faculties are failing . . .
May we sing your praises all our days.

God of wisdom, in the cross you reconciled your creation to you.
Bring into your peace all who have died . . .
May we come to behold the fullness of your glory.

Year C

When we call you answer
Great is your glory.

Master, you still the raging waters.
Come to your Church and speak your words of peace to disputes and
    fears . . .
Deepen our faith to trust in your providence.

Master, you bring calm to the storm.
Come to your world and speak your words of justice to conflicts . . .
Let all peoples praise you.

Master, you bring people together in love.
Come to our homes and speak your words of comfort and joy . . .
Give stability and security to all parents and children.

Master, you hear our cries of desperation.
Come to us in all our weakness and speak your words of compassion
    and mercy . . .
Relieve our anxious hearts with the gift of your tranquil presence.

Master, you delight our hope with visions of your heavenly glory.
Come to our dying and speak your words of salvation . . .
By your will we have life and are brought to new life.

Sunday next before Lent

Year A

Lord of glory
We behold the mystery of your love.

Lord, it is good for us to come into your presence.
Silence our babbling mouths that your Church may hear your Word . . .
Inspire us with the vision of your beloved Son.

Lord, on the mountain Moses waited for your commandments.
Raise up prophetic voices to give sound counsel to world leaders . . .
Direct this and every nation in the path of peace with justice.

Lord, your Son took Peter, James and John to witness the revelation of
    your love.
Fill our hearts with rejoicing and humble thanksgiving . . .
With friends and strangers, unite us in the household of your Kingdom.

Lord, you bring light to places in darkness and hope to all who despair.
Be with all whose journey is hard and unremitting . . .
From the heights of the mountain refresh and renew our flagging spirits.

Lord, hope springs eternal with you.
Receive with your transforming love those who have died . . .
May the brightness radiating from your mystery be our final refuge.

Year B

Lord of glory
We behold the mystery of your love.

With the eyes of faith, deepen our vision, O Lord, that we may see
more fully the splendour of your creation.
Bathe your Church in your glory and light . . .
Renew our commitment to tell of your wonders.

With the eyes of faith, reveal anew the challenge of your Kingdom.
Give to political leaders zeal for your justice and harmony . . .
Unite all people in common purpose and peace.

With the eyes of faith, open our sight to the good in our neighbours of
all ages.
We give thanks for those whose hopefulness transforms everyone they
meet . . .
Give us thankful hearts with which to praise you.

With the eyes of faith, we hold before you all who feel under a cloud of
despair or anxiety.
Bless all who are ill . . .
Enfold us in your love.

With the eyes of faith, grant us to trust in your unfailing promise of
salvation.
We commit to you all who have died . . .
Christ, risen and enthroned in majesty, raise us all to be with you for
ever.

Year C

Lord of glory
We behold the mystery of your love.

Master, Chosen One, your radiant glory fills your Church with hope and expectation.
Transform our actions as we listen to and wait upon your presence . . .
Make us a people prepared to declare your love with boldness and trust.

Master, Chosen One, on the mountain the world was revealed to be subject to your rule.
We entrust to you the nations of the earth and all who govern . . .
Transform our structures with your justice and peace.

Master, Chosen One, Peter rushed to preserve the moment of your transfiguration.
Capture our hearts for your Kingdom . . .
Make us agents of transformation in public and private relationships.

Master, Chosen One, on coming down from the mountain you healed the boy held in the grip of convulsions.
Pour out your transforming love on all who cry for release from their sufferings . . .
Set us free to sing your praises.

Master, Chosen One, you spoke with the ancient prophets of your impending passion and resurrection.
Transform our fear and bring us to trust in you . . .
Bring us with all the departed to your eternal city.

Ash Wednesday

Years A, B and C

In your loving-kindness, O God
Have mercy and hear our prayer.

Merciful Lord, cleanse our hearts that we may offer praise worthy of
your name.
Give to your Church true penitence and mourning for the sins that
would drive a wedge between who we are and all you would have us
become . . .
Wash us and we shall be clean.

Gracious Lord, you call us to a justice that leaves no one excluded or
oppressed.
Sound the trumpet of alarm to waken leaders and governments to the
cries of all afflicted . . .
May your light break forth with joy and gladness for all people.

God of compassion, travel with us through this season of fasting.
Refocus our vision on your eternal promises . . .
As we let go of our clinging to false treasures so may we find riches
beyond measure.

Lord, at your word we find release from all that would hold us captive.
Bring rejoicing to those in any kind of sorrow . . .
Deliver us, O God of our salvation.

Ash Wednesday

Eternal Lord, from dust we came and to dust we shall return.
In sure and certain hope of your risen Son,
hear us as we commend to you those who have died . . .
Bring us at the last to the glory of your eternal Kingdom.

Lent 1

Year A

In your loving-kindness, O God
Have mercy and hear our prayer.

God of enduring majesty, in the wilderness your Son was subjected to
repeated temptation to deny you.
Give to your Church the fortitude it needs to give faithful witness to
your abundant grace . . .
May the true of heart shout for joy.

From the dizzy heights of achievement and effort, false worship was
evoked.
Forgive our pride and arrogance when we are tempted to bow down
before images of our own making . . .
Give humility to all with power to worship you alone.

From the Temple pinnacle recklessness and folly were encouraged.
Bring wisdom to all whose plans strain what is sustainable and
fruitful . . .
Prevent us, O Lord, from seeking to test your providential care.

Hungry and thirsty, your Son was taken to the limits of his endurance.
Be with all whose spirits are breaking and whose strength is sapped . . .
May your Word uphold and strengthen us in all adversity.

With Adam all die, but in Christ new life is opened to us.
In this trust we remember with thanksgiving all who have died . . .
Bring us to dwell with you for ever.

Year B

God of our salvation
We trust in your promise.

God of grace, your Kingdom draws near to us in your Son.
Increase in your Church trust in the fulfilment of your promises . . .
Fill our hearts with the joy of your good news announced to us.

God of grace, prophetic witness led to John being arrested.
Be with all who courageously make a stand for justice and liberty . . .
Give us faith to trust in the victory of right.

God of grace, you set the world in a universe of awesome wonder.
Awaken all peoples to the urgent need for ecological balance . . .
In your mercy bring humanity back from the brink of self-destruction.

God of grace, in the wilderness your Son had to face the limits of
    humanity.
Hold in your tender care all who suffer . . .
We put our trust in you, O Lord.

God of grace, in baptism we are united with Christ's death and
    resurrection.
In this hope we commend to you all who have died . . .
May we too come to enjoy the benefits of your beloved.

Year C

God our refuge and stronghold
We put our trust in your salvation.

Lord Jesus, for forty days you fasted and were tested to your core.
Give your Church the faith to set aside all that masks the spiritual
struggles within . . .
We will worship you with all our heart and soul and strength.

Lord Jesus, in the wilderness you went without securities and confronted
your fears.
Give to the nations courage to put away the politics of suspicion and
panic . . .
Protect us from all that seeks to divide and exploit the vulnerable.

Lord Jesus, you placed yourself at the mercy of hunger and weakness.
Give to the satisfied concern and compassion for those who are not sure
of their next meal . . .
Preserve us from gluttony and excessive living.

Lord Jesus, you endured the dry places and the discomfort of stones for
your bed.
Give to all who feel their life is parched the refreshment of your living
stream . . .
Bring us to trust in your mercy.

Lord Jesus, alone you became at one with the Father and the Spirit.
Be with us that we may enter the silence of your eternity . . .
As we call on your name, bring us to your salvation.

Lent 2

———————

Year A

In your loving-kindness, O God
Have mercy and hear our prayer.

Lord, in the night-time of his questing, Nicodemus came to your Son
   wondering and puzzling over all he had seen.
Come to your Church and meet us as we seek to deepen our faith . . .
Fill with your Spirit all who have been baptized in your name.

In Abraham we share a common heritage with people of different races,
   languages and creeds.
Unite all people in a common humanity . . .
Watch over the nations and bless the families of the earth.

Preserve us, O Lord, from all that is evil and would do us harm.
Increase in us your gift of grace and charity . . .
Lift our gaze to the heights of your presence.

In the night-time of our despair we call to you for help, for relief, for
   healing.
Be with all who long for reprieve in their sufferings . . .
Restore within us hope in you.

Lord, you came not to condemn but to save; to give life to the dead.
Look with mercy upon the children of your promise who have departed
   this life . . .
Grant eternal life to all who trust in you.

Year B

God of our salvation
We trust in your promise.

Jesus, Saviour of the world, you embraced the way of sacrificial love.
Give your Church faith and courage to follow you wherever it may
    lead . . .
Pour us out as a libation in your service.

Jesus, Saviour of the world, raise up leaders who will dedicate themselves
    to the common good.
In the heat of conflicting convictions keep them in truth and integrity . . .
May your justice flow.

Jesus, Saviour of the world, in you all peoples are one.
Strengthen the bonds that create a cohesive and peaceful society . . .
We pray for centres of community life.

Jesus, Saviour of the world, we look to you in our hour of need.
Pour out your blessing on all who are ill or weakened . . .
Fill our hearts with your joy and gladness.

Jesus, Saviour of the world, in you we find truth and life.
Do not be ashamed of us at the hour of our death . . .
When you come in your glory, draw us home to be with you.

Year C

God our refuge and stronghold
We put our trust in your salvation.

Blessed are you, O Lord, for you draw all people to you.
Give to your Church the same passion, that everyone may find a place
  within its embrace . . .
Give grace that we may stand firm in you.

Blessed are you, O Lord, for you challenge leaders with your truth and
  justice.
Give to all who govern wisdom to seek your peace . . .
Strengthen the arm of all who defend the weak and persecuted.

Blessed are you, O Lord, for you gather disparate and diverse people
  into community.
Give to our society vision to be inclusive and open . . .
Transform our bodies from humiliation to glory.

Blessed are you, O Lord, for you proclaim release and healing.
Give to all who suffer cause for hope in and beyond their sufferings . . .
We will rejoice and be glad in you.

Blessed are you, O Lord, for you complete your work in rising from the
  grave.
Give this hope to all who have died . . .
Bring us to the fulfilment of our citizenship of heaven.

Lent 3

Year A

In your loving-kindness, O God
Have mercy and hear our prayer.

Lord, you draw near and meet us when we are thirsty and weary.
You give to your people living water gushing up to eternal life . . .
Revive and refresh your Church to tell of your wonders.

Lord, in communities around the world, some turn on taps but for many
 gathering water is a daily chore.
Bless the work of development agencies in improving access to clean
 water and sanitation . . .
With you, O Lord, is the well of life.

Lord, in adversity and under pressure we become quarrelsome and turn
 on you.
Teach us to sing your praises when things go well and when times are
 difficult . . .
In your mercy you turn sorrow into dancing.

Lord, you strengthen the weak and give courage to the faint of heart.
Be with all whose endurance is being tested to its limits . . .
Restore our hope in your loving presence.

Lord, you prove your love for us in the death and resurrection of your
 Son.
Gather for eternal life all who have died hoping in you . . .
Jesus, Saviour of the world, we trust in your eternal salvation.

Year B

God of our salvation
We trust in your promise.

Lord, you come to your Temple with zeal and indignation.
Come to your Church and drive from it all false piety and misguided
    priorities . . .
May our words, thoughts and deeds be acceptable in your sight.

Lord, you come to places of power and some are affronted at your
    audacity.
Open the hearts of all in leadership to the challenge of your
    Kingdom . . .
Revive us in your justice.

Lord, you come to traders with a vision that extends beyond profit.
Keep us mindful of the conditions of production and social effects of
    what we consume . . .
Balance all our trading with your fairness and equity.

Lord, you come to our lives with compassion and searching judgement.
In our frailty give us time to reflect on what is amiss and in repentance
    to seek your restoring grace . . .
Create in us a fitting dwelling-place for your glory.

Lord, you come with the promise of your resurrection.
Give comfort and hope to all who mourn . . .
Bring us to new life with you.

Year C

God our refuge and stronghold
We put our trust in your salvation.

Judge eternal, give to your Church a penitent and contrite heart.
Where it is dry, refresh it; where it fails to bear fruit, renew it . . .
Make us agents of your transforming love.

Judge eternal, give to all in power awareness of the awesome
    responsibility they carry.
Inspire them to forsake ways that oppress by intent or omission . . .
Make us agents of your justice and peace.

Judge eternal, give to all people vision to shape our communities as
    places where all can delight and flourish.
Nurture the young, care for the infirm, bring hope to all who
    struggle . . .
Make us agents of your generosity.

Judge eternal, give to all who are weary and weighed down relief in
    their sufferings.
Bless them by your life-giving presence . . .
Make us agents of your wholeness and healing.

Judge eternal, give to all who journey under the cloud of death a
    glimpse of your light and life.
Hold all who weep and mourn . . .
Make us ready to share in the glory of your eternity.

Lent 4

Year A

In your loving-kindness, O God
Have mercy and hear our prayer.

Jesus, light of the world, open the eyes of your Church to the wonders
of your saving love.
May we delight in all whose works are good and right and true . . .
Lord, we believe and worship your holy name.

Jesus, light of the world, you look on the heart and not merely on
outward appearance.
Expose the motives of all who lead and seek to shape our common
life . . .
Bring peace with justice.

Jesus, light of the world, be with all whose eyesight is impaired.
We pray for Guide Dogs for the Blind, and all who provide support to
the blind and partially sighted . . .
Teach us to look beyond appearance and the vanities that cloud our
vision.

Jesus, light of the world, shine your light into the darkness of disease and
troubles of the mind . . .
In your tender compassion, revive and refresh our souls.

Jesus, light of the world, you lead us through the valley of the shadow
of death, and we will fear no evil.
Hear us as we remember before you all who have died . . .
Bring us to dwell in your house for ever.

Year B

God of our salvation
We trust in your promise.

Loving Lord Jesus, on the cross you revealed the Father's heart.
As we lift high the cross may we never be ashamed of its message of
  salvation . . .
Give grace to your Church to proclaim your glory.

Loving Lord Jesus, you confront our fears and expose the secrets of our
  hearts.
Lighten the path of those to whom we give the responsibility of
  government . . .
May we honour that which is true and right.

Loving Lord Jesus, Moses gave the sign of the serpent for healing.
Bless all involved in pharmaceutical research . . .
We give thanks for the benefits of the application of science.

Loving Lord Jesus, you reached out to all who came to you by day and
  by night.
Hear our prayers for all in need of your healing touch . . .
Send forth your word and we shall be restored to wholeness in you.

Loving Lord Jesus, you are rich in mercy and we depend on your grace
  alone to save us.
In this hope we commend to you all who have died . . .
Hold your cross before us that we may have eternal life.

Year C

God our refuge and stronghold
We put our trust in your salvation.

God of compassion and mercy, you are ready to forgive and restore us
    long before we repent.
Turn your Church to emulate your generous heart . . .
Fill us with your gracious love.

God of compassion and mercy, you weep when brothers and sisters in
    humanity quarrel and are beset by grudges.
Set us free to delight in redemption over vengeance . . .
Forgive all squandering of your rich bounty.

God of compassion and mercy, you give sufficient for all to be full.
Release our selfish grasp on the fruits of the earth and commerce . . .
Transform unjust structures in trading and governance.

God of compassion and mercy, you hear the cry of the distressed and
    destitute.
Come to greet us as we turn to you in our anxiety . . .
Speak your words of blessing and life.

God of compassion and mercy, in Christ you reconcile the world to
    yourself.
Remember in love all who have died . . .
Bring us with them to the new creation in your Son.

Mothering Sunday
(Alternative Lent 4)

―――◆◆◆―――

Years A, B and C

Let your steadfast love be upon us, O Lord
We will exult and rejoice in you.

Eternal God, you are constant with your people.
Like a mother you draw all your children to your heart . . .
Guide us in the ways of truth that we may rejoice in your bountiful
goodness.

Holy God, your presence is always before us.
We give thanks for all who have nurtured us and helped us grow in
faith and trust . . .
Bless all midwives of the gospel.
Increase your Church in hope and courage to proclaim your love.

God our Father and Mother, you allow us to share in your creative
purpose.
Sustain and keep all parents and children,
that through the love that is shared our lives may be blessed . . .
Be with all for whom this day brings pain and regret to the fore.
Transform us through your brooding grace.

God our succour and protector,
in times of plenty and need, you cradle our life in your hands.
We entrust to your care all in any kind of need . . .
Encircle them with your love and keep them ever within your tender
mercy.

From the cross your Son commended his mother to the care of his
beloved disciple.
Hear the cry of all who mourn.
Comfort and sustain them in their grief . . .
Bring us to rejoice with you in the New Jerusalem, our heavenly home.

Lent 5 – Passion Sunday

Year A

In your loving-kindness, O God
Have mercy and hear our prayer.

Jesus, our resurrection and our life, raise our vision and centre it on your
   eternity.
Breathe into your Church the vitality of your Spirit . . .
Make us a holy dwelling place for you.

Jesus, our resurrection and our life, look with compassion on your
   world.
Make the dry bones of political intrigue come to life that all may dance
   in your freedom . . .
Loose the bonds of corruption and set free all that enhances godly living.

Jesus, our resurrection and our life, draw together into one body
   dispersed and fractured peoples.
Connect the strands of society uniting people of all races, ages and
   gender . . .
Dwell among us, Lord, that we may behold your glory.

Jesus, our resurrection and our life, be with all who are ill in mind or
   body . . .
Reveal your glory in our frailty.

Jesus, our resurrection and our life, you restore life where it has been
   lost,
and we rejoice in the warmth of your love . . .
May we hear you call us from the place of death to delight in your new
   creation.

Year B

God of our salvation
We trust in your promise.

You come to meet us, O Lord, long before we search for you.
Make your Church a gateway to encountering your presence and
   glory . . .
May we show forth your love and always direct hearts to you.

You come to meet us, O Lord, amidst the struggles and tensions of
   life.
Give all people courage to stand for justice and peace . . .
Bring in your Kingdom of truth and liberty.

You come to meet us, O Lord, in moments of faithfulness and failure.
Give us grace to confront the darkness within and to embrace your new
   life . . .
Help victims and offenders to be set free from all that burdens them.

You come to meet us, O Lord, in strength and weakness.
As you shared our frailty, give comfort to all in distress or adversity . . .
In all our infirmity we share in your passion.

You come to meet us, O Lord, in your cross and resurrection.
Draw to yourself all who have died . . .
As we sing the praise of him who died, so may we come to triumph in
   his victory.

Year C

God our refuge and stronghold
We put our trust in your salvation.

Christ Jesus, at dinner with friends Mary anointed you in anticipation of
your forthcoming passion.
Inspire your Church with this profligate love . . .
Delight us with the fragrance of true devotion to you.

Christ Jesus, Judas and Lazarus shared your company.
Confront all who sit in parliaments and councils with the call for honesty
and integrity . . .
Keep us hopeful and respectful.

Christ Jesus, Martha served at table ensuring guests were fed.
Bless all whose work is overlooked and unregarded . . .
Let none be despised or dishonoured.

Christ Jesus, you acknowledged that the poor will always be with us.
As we recognize the limits to our agency, anoint with your Holy Spirit
all in need . . .
In our frailty give us grace to praise you.

Christ Jesus, everything we have is of little worth next to the value of
knowing you.
Present to all who have died your heavenly prize . . .
May we with them attain the resurrection to come.

Palm Sunday

———•◆•———

Year A

Hosanna to the Son of David!
Hosanna in the highest heaven!

Lord Jesus Christ, you humbled yourself and became as nothing for our
    redemption.
Give to your Church the servant mind to display your grace and
    mercy . . .
We bow the knee and confess your name.

Lord Jesus Christ, on this day the crowd shouted praises,
but in just a few days they turned on you.
We pray for all at the mercy of fickle popularity . . .
Give governments strength and courage to hold to what is true and
    right.

Lord Jesus Christ, as the crowd spread their cloaks and waved tree
    branches in your honour, we give thanks for the occasions that fill
    us with joy at being alive . . .
Draw us closer to one another and to you.

Lord Jesus Christ, in your passion we see our human frailty.
Be with all whose endurance is strained and spirit is weakened by their
    ailments . . .
Sustain the weary with your eternal word.

Lord Jesus Christ, you shared our life even to the point of death.
Gather to yourself in gentleness and peace all who have died . . .
As you are highly exalted so may we come to share in your eternal
    Kingdom.

Year B

Give thanks to the Lord
His mercy endures for ever.

Blessed are you, O Lord, the king who rides on the colt of a donkey.
We lay before you our lives dedicated to your service . . .
Give your Church grace to sing your praises in word and deed.

Blessed are you, O Lord, the servant king.
We lay before you the decisions and choices we must make . . .
Give us grace to use the power we have for the benefit of all.

Blessed are you, O Lord, friend of rich and poor.
We lay before you our friendships and those we find difficult to be
    with . . .
Give us grace to delight in intimacy shared.

Blessed are you, O Lord, suffering servant.
We lay before you the sick and dying . . .
Give us hope to find a voice to sing your praise.

Blessed are you, O Lord, crucified king.
We lay before you all who have died . . .
Give life eternal to all whose trust is in you.

Year C

I will give thanks to the Lord
For you answer our prayer.

With shouts of joy and jubilation the crowd announced your triumphal
    entry to the city.
Fill your Church with these praises . . .
Keep us steadfast in times of trouble and peace.

With shouts of anger and hatred the crowd called for your death.
Strengthen the hand of all who lead not to abuse their power . . .
Preserve us from injustice.

With shouts of horror and defiance your disciples swore allegiance and
    loyalty.
Give courage to all whose fidelity is tested against popularity . . .
Save us from betrayal and deceit.

With shouts of anguish and terror frightened friends looked on powerless
    and impotent.
Be with all who stare into the darkness of anxiety . . .
Shine the light of your hope to illumine the shadows of despair.

With shouts of grief and desolation your mother and closest companions
    received your lifeless body.
Be alongside all who weep by the body of one they love . . .
Bring us to the joy that comes with the first light of the new day.

Monday of Holy Week

Years A, B and C

With you is the well of life
In your light we shall see light.

Jesus, facing plots of murder and treachery, Mary anointed you with
  fragrant oil.
May its sweet smell fill your Church with your grace in the face of
  adversity . . .
As your love reaches to the heavens so may we rise to sing your praises.

Jesus, servant Lord, bring in your justice to the nations of the earth.
Lighten our path for the good of all . . .
Bring peace to troubled places.

Jesus, as Judas sneered at Mary's gift,
restore the dignity and self-worth of all eaten by bitterness and hatred . . .
Do not let wickedness push any aside.

Jesus, you are tender and gentle with the bruised and frail.
Be with any nearing exhaustion and enduring severe strain . . .
Take them by your hand and keep them.

Jesus, you raised Lazarus to life and promised new life to all who trust in
  you.
Remember for good your servants departed this life . . .
Pour out your life-giving Spirit.

Tuesday of Holy Week

Years A, B and C

With you is the well of life
In your light we shall see light.

Lord, your foolishness is wiser than our wisdom
and your weakness stronger than human strength.
May your Church glorify your name throughout the earth . . .
Give grace to your people to help all who wish to see Jesus to find him.

Lord, guide our steps by the light of your love.
Let not the darkness overtake us . . .
As we proclaim your cross, so may we declare your power and wisdom.

Lord, you are our hope.
Be with all losing heart, who feel their labour is in vain . . .
Deliver us in your righteousness.

Lord, come to the aid of all who wait on you with patience and trust,
and all agitated in their frustration and anxiety . . .
Be with all who seek salvation from this hour.

Lord, judge of the world, draw to yourself all who have died . . .
Bring to your eternity all who trust in you.

Wednesday of Holy Week

Years A, B and C

With you is the well of life
In your light we shall see light.

Lord, your Son persevered and endured the cross for our redemption.
As we prepare to commemorate again the events of his saving passion,
   keep your Church steadfast in its faith . . .
Preserve us, O Lord, from losing heart.

Lord, your Son knew the darkness at work in Judas' heart.
Forgive the sins that will betray and condemn some for others' gain . . .
Draw us back from taking pleasure in the misfortunes of any.

Lord, your Son shared table fellowship with his friends and those closest
   to him.
Draw us closer to one another and to you as we break bread together . . .
Restore us in your image, O God.

Lord, your Son was troubled in spirit and knew the anguish of facing
   human mortality.
Be with all who cry to you and make haste to help them . . .
Sustain us, O Lord, with your Word of life.

Lord, your Son proclaimed your glory in the face of death.
Deliver us at the hour of our death . . .
Bring us to say 'Great is the Lord'.

Maundy Thursday

Years A, B and C

Lord, we will lift up the cup of salvation
And call upon your name.

Jesus, servant Lord, in your final moments with your disciples you chose
to give an example of loving service.
Fill your Church with this servant heart . . .
May the love we display be worthy of your calling and name.

Jesus, servant Lord, in explaining your actions to bemused disciples you
reminded them that all authority is derived from you.
Give all who lead and govern due humility in their position . . .
Prevent all with power from becoming puffed up and overbearing.

Jesus, servant Lord, in taking the bread and cup you gave a feast in
remembrance of you.
Bind together all who share in this fellowship and communion . . .
Keep us from betraying our hope in you.

Jesus, servant Lord, in agony in the garden you shared with all who face
anguish and whose hearts are troubled . . .
With your broken bread and blood outpoured we hold before your
healing grace our pains and sorrows.

Jesus, servant Lord, as we eat this bread and drink this cup we proclaim
your death until you come again.
Draw to yourself all who have died . . .
Glorify your name and bring us to life with you.

Good Friday

Lord, we will lift your name on high
And praise you before all people.

Jesus, for us and for our salvation,
you were despised and rejected.
May your passion turn our faltering hearts to the depth and breadth and
height of your love.

Jesus, for us and for our salvation,
you were crushed by a perversion of justice.
Be with the oppressed and those rightly convicted.
Turn our hearts in penitence for the sins that separate us from one
another and from you.

Jesus, for us and for our salvation,
you became a man of suffering and acquainted with infirmity.
As you take our pains and diseases upon yourself,
so may we know your power to bring us to wholeness and peace.

Jesus, for us and for our salvation,
you were laid in a borrowed tomb and dwelt in the place of silence.
Lamb of God, gather to yourself all who have died.

In your cross, O Lord, we glory and we enthrone you on our praises.
For you are the Holy One and in you alone we place our trust and
hope.

Easter Day

Year A

Risen Lord
Fill our hearts with Easter joy.

Living Lord, at the dawn of day the earth was shaken by your
    life-restoring power.
Shake your Church today by this seismic news . . .
Send us out to tell of your wonder.

Living Lord, your resurrection startled guards and friends alike.
Shatter the fears that stifle our politics . . .
Breathe new life into our common living.

Living Lord, you make no distinctions between people.
Transform the narrowness of our vision and judgement . . .
Meet us and greet us in our journey together.

Living Lord, your mercy endures for ever.
Strengthen and sustain all whose spirits are weak
and whose lives are gripped by pain or distress . . .
We will give you thanks for your great goodness.

Living Lord, confused friends left your empty tomb in both fear and
    great joy.
We hold before you the sadness of loss and the joy of our hope in
    you . . .
Raise us all to share in your glory.

Year B

Sing to the Lord a new song
For he has done marvellous things.

Risen Lord, in the early morning freshness, with spices to anoint,
three friends approached your empty tomb.
May your Easter rising continue to surprise your Church with new life
    and hope . . .
Shape us as witnesses of your grace and power.

Risen Lord, news of your rising was greeted with alarm and fear.
Free us from all that shrouds your people in death and despair . . .
Set our hearts at peace with thanksgiving.

Risen Lord, your appearing changed lives and made witnesses from
    broken people.
Give hope to all who seek your transforming love . . .
Form us in your grace and likeness.

Risen Lord, you make the day dawn with promise.
Raise the spirits of all who are ill . . .
Strengthen and uphold them in your life and love.

Risen Lord, in your rising we see salvation.
Draw to yourself all who have died . . .
Wipe away tears from our eyes that we may rejoice and be glad in you.

Year C

Give thanks to the Lord
Rejoice and praise his name.

Lord of life, in rising from the dead you bring a hope that reaches
  beyond this life.
Fill your Church with this vibrancy that it may proclaim anew your
  salvation . . .
Raise our sights beyond the limits of our expectation.

Lord of life, you love all people equally.
Leave no place for the hatreds that divide and oppress . . .
Bind us together as fellow citizens of your Kingdom.

Lord of life, you chose to reveal your rising to the women first.
Forgive the prejudices that dismiss the witness of those you make
  unlikely messengers . . .
Bring new life to all our relationships.

Lord of life, you offer a vision of new heavens and a new earth.
Keep from despair all who carry heavy burdens of mind or body . . .
Strengthen and uphold them in all their sufferings.

Lord of life, your resurrection startled and amazed grief-stricken friends.
In your love raise all who have died . . .
Make our song the alleluias of heaven.

Easter 2

Year A

Risen Lord
Fill our hearts with Easter joy.

Lord Jesus Christ, you appeared to your disciples and brought them
    peace.
May your Church rejoice in your presence and life-giving Spirit . . .
Bring us through our doubts to proclaim you as Lord and God.

Lord Jesus Christ, your resurrection broke the hold of death.
Set free all with responsibility for government from fears that would
    impoverish the spirit . . .
Bring all nations to rejoice in your freedom.

Lord Jesus Christ, you sent your disciples as apostles of forgiveness and
    penitence.
Turn our hearts from the evil we do and the good we do not do . . .
Set us free from the weight of sin that clings so persistently.

Lord Jesus Christ, you desire our good above all other and speak
    tenderly to the afflicted.
Hold close to you those whose needs we bring before you . . .
Bring us through times of trial to praise and glorify your name.

Lord Jesus Christ, you were handed over and crucified for our salvation.
Bring to your inheritance all who died trusting in this hope . . .
Grant life in your name.

Year B

Sing to the Lord a new song
For he has done marvellous things.

Lord Jesus, you announce peace to your disciples.
Breathe into your Church the Holy Spirit . . .
Give faith for doubt and boldness to fainting hearts.

Lord Jesus, you announce peace to your world.
Breathe upon the nations desire for harmony and concord . . .
Strengthen the fearful and all who seek to reconcile places of conflict.

Lord Jesus, you announce peace to our communities.
Breathe upon our common life your generosity . . .
In your grace open our hearts to share of our riches and poverty.

Lord Jesus, you announce peace to injured and battered peoples.
Breathe upon all in special need your healing presence . . .
Anoint us all in your great goodness.

Lord Jesus, you announce peace in the face of death.
Breathe upon all who have died your life and forgiveness . . .
Bring light to the darkness of death and rejoicing to the place of
    tears.

Year C

Give thanks to the Lord
Rejoice and praise his name.

Jesus come among us.
Breathe new life into your Church . . .
Give us grace to proclaim you as our Lord and God.

Jesus come among us.
Take away the fear that closes doors and shuts some out . . .
Give us grace to embrace strangers and friends with charity and love.

Jesus come among us.
Open our voices to speak with courage where evil would prefer
    silence . . .
Give us grace to strive for justice.

Jesus come among us.
Pour out your Holy Spirit on all in need of release from guilt and past
    mistakes . . .
Give us grace to announce your healing and liberation.

Jesus come among us.
Come in glory for all who have died . . .
Give life in your name.

Easter 3

Year A

Risen Lord
Fill our hearts with Easter joy.

Risen Lord, you set ablaze the hearts of your disciples with awe and
wonder at your resurrection.
Open the eyes of your Church to this astounding news . . .
Fill our voices with joy that you are risen indeed.

Risen Lord, you see and judge the motives of rulers and leaders.
Raise up and sustain with your Holy Spirit people of integrity for the
responsibilities of government . . .
Bring peace and justice to flourish.

Risen Lord, you drew alongside confused disciples as they journeyed to
Emmaus.
Give grace to all who accompany others in their searching . . .
For all who share their table and offer hospitality, we give you thanks.

Risen Lord, you incline your ear to all who call upon you.
Free us from the bonds that restrict our movement and dampen our
praises . . .
Bless all who set their hope and trust on you.

Risen Lord, you came to your disciples in the darkness and impaired
vision of their grief.
Come close to all whose hearts are anguished by loss . . .
Bring us to rejoice in your eternal Kingdom.

Year B

Sing to the Lord a new song
For he has done marvellous things.

Holy and righteous one, open the mind of your Church to the
fulfilment of your promise beyond our imagining.
Give us faith to trust in your life-restoring power . . .
Raise up faithful witnesses to proclaim the wonders of your love.

Holy and righteous one, inspire legislators to defend the dignity of all life.
May no one be regarded as being of less worth . . .
Teach us to honour all people as your children.

Holy and righteous one, be with all who teach.
Sharpen our minds on the wonders of your creation . . .
Nurture wisdom and train us to use the gifts you give.

Holy and righteous one, we bring before you all who seek your healing
grace.
Pour upon them your consolation . . .
Strengthen the faint-hearted and give peace to the dying.

Holy and righteous one, you hold before us a promise of great hope.
Bring us to share in the life of your redeemed . . .
Author of life, we look to the final revelation of your eternity.

Year C

Give thanks to the Lord
Rejoice and praise his name.

At breakfast by the seashore, Lord Jesus, you recommissioned your
disciples.
Re-energize your Church to proclaim your resurrection and truth . . .
Turn the catchless night into a teeming body of praise.

In the safety of familiar company, Lord Jesus, you restored Simon Peter
in your service.
Forgive our faltering steps and denials of your ways under pressure . . .
Give us grace and courage to follow you in our common life.

On the road to Damascus, Lord Jesus, you confronted Saul with his
rebellious hatred.
Turn the hearts of all who oppress through distortions of self-image and
identity . . .
Give peace to troubled hearts and lives.

With the embrace of charity, Lord Jesus, you sent Ananias to restore
Saul's sight.
Send your liberating and transforming Spirit on all who suffer restrictions
of mind, body or spirit . . .
Strengthen them with your redeeming love.

From the darkness of death, Lord Jesus, you were raised to life.
Shine this light on all who have died and those who grieve for them . . .
Give us faith to trust in your salvation.

Easter 4

Year A

Risen Lord
Fill our hearts with Easter joy.

God of our salvation, you open your life to our lives and we rejoice in
　　your hospitality.
Keep your Church abounding in this generous heart . . .
Our hearts leap for joy when we hear you call.

God of our salvation, inspire leaders to be true shepherds of your
　　people;
to exercise their power for the mutual benefit of all . . .
Bind together in a common humanity people of every race and
　　language.

God of our salvation, your grace entices us to share the fruits of your
　　goodness.
Open the fortresses we construct to shut others out that we may
　　celebrate the life you bring . . .
Revive our disparate souls.

God of our salvation, you still the troubled waters and lead us to places
　　of refreshment and tranquillity.
Anoint with your peace all in need of your healing touch . . .
Protect and keep the sheep of your pasture.

God of our salvation, gather to your eternal sheepfold all who have
　　died . . .
Grant that we may all dwell in your house for ever.

Year B

Sing to the Lord a new song
For he has done marvellous things.

Jesus, Good Shepherd, we come to you, the true guardian of our souls.
Keep your Church focused firmly on you and your Kingdom . . .
Draw us closer in unity and fellowship in your name.

Jesus, Good Shepherd, we come to you, our true defence.
Give us courage to place our trust in following your way of peace . . .
Draw the nations closer in a commonwealth of shared humanity.

Jesus, Good Shepherd, we come to you, the true owner of all wealth.
Open the hearts and purses of all, that as we have richly received so we
    may be generous in our giving . . .
Raise benefactors who can enable all that delights and liberates.

Jesus, Good Shepherd, we come to you with the injured and the weak.
Protect and hold in your love all who cry to you in their need . . .
Revive us in your mercy.

Jesus, Good Shepherd, you lay down your life for our salvation.
Gather us in our final hour to your eternal fold . . .
As you know us, so may we hear you call us by name in your
    Kingdom.

Year C

Give thanks to the Lord
Rejoice and praise his name.

Lord Jesus, anointed at your baptism, you fulfil our hopes beyond our
    imagining.
Gather into your Church all who hear and respond to your call . . .
Teach us how to be people of your redemption.

Lord Jesus, you showed in signs and wonders your saving love.
Transform our aspirations to recognize and embrace your dawning
    Kingdom . . .
Give to leaders and governments vision to pursue your peace.

Lord Jesus, you give diverse gifts so that all may contribute to the
    common good.
Give us grace to honour and delight in the talents shared . . .
Shape us together for your glory.

Lord Jesus, the sick and infirm were brought to you for healing.
We hold before your tender love all who need your healing touch
    today . . .
Pour upon them your blessing.

Lord Jesus, salvation belongs to you and you give eternal life.
We commend to you those who have died . . .
Bring us to rejoice with the great multitude of heaven.

Easter 5

Year A

Risen Lord
Fill our hearts with Easter joy.

Lord, our way, our truth, our life,
in you the mystery of eternity is opened and we behold your glory.
Inspire your Church with this vision and build it into a spiritual house
for you . . .
Give us grace to grow into salvation.

Lord, our way, our truth, our life,
you cast out fear and in trusting in you all people rejoice.
Expand the vision of political leaders to embrace respect and dignity for
all . . .
Grant that our actions may proclaim life in its fullness.

Lord, our way, our truth, our life,
move between us and unite all people into a community as your beloved
children.
Strengthen the bonds that make for cohesive living . . .
Called by you, shape us as people of your promise.

Lord, our way, our truth, our life,
in you our troubled hearts are eased and we are enfolded in your
love.
Hear our prayer for all whom we name before you . . .
May the light of your countenance give hope and peace.

Lord, our way, our truth, our life,
you prepare a place for us and take us to be with you for ever.
Carry to yourself all who have died . . .
Lord Jesus, receive our spirits.

Year B

Sing to the Lord a new song
For he has done marvellous things.

Jesus, you are the vine and we your branches.
Keep us abiding in your life and love . . .
Prune and tend your Church that it may bear fruitful disciples of your
    grace.

Jesus, the Ethiopian official sought to understand your good news.
Expand the hearts and minds of all in authority to pursue truth and
    justice . . .
Bring reason for all people to rejoice.

Jesus, your love sets our hearts ablaze.
Open the hearts of all people to reflect this love in ways that nurture
    and foster character . . .
Strengthen all who support parenting and provide guidance for the
    young.

Jesus, your love precedes us and we respond with adoration and praise.
Give to all who are afflicted grace to bathe in this affection . . .
Raise us to delight in your loving purposes through good times and bad.

Jesus, we are made for your love.
Do not forget the children you have made . . .
May we all come to abide with you for ever.

Year C

Give thanks to the Lord
Rejoice and praise his name.

God of love, hours before betrayal and arrest your Son commanded his
　disciples to love.
Make this our first thought and intent . . .
Fill your Church with the gift of your abiding grace.

God of love, you desire that humanity should dwell together in unity
　and peace.
Heal us of the anger and bitterness in which violence and hatred
　breed . . .
Teach us the way of self-giving love.

God of love, you challenge us to embrace a broad community.
Silence the narrowness of our charity . . .
Give us a heart to praise you in thought and deed.

God of love, you show compassion and mercy to all your children.
Embrace in your love all who cry for relief in their suffering . . .
Revive our longing hearts.

God of love, in the resurrection of Christ Jesus you open to all people
　the gates of your New Jerusalem.
Welcome to your heavenly city all who have died . . .
Take away the heartache of grief and replace it with the joy of your
　eternity.

Easter 6

Year A

Risen Lord
Fill our hearts with Easter joy.

Love of the Father, love of the Son, abide in your Church.
Pour out your Holy Spirit of truth and challenge the narrowness of our
   vision and charity . . .
We join our praises with all who worship and adore you, whether
   known or unknown.

Loving Father, you challenge the structures of the world with a justice
   that reaches beyond self-interest.
Hold before us the standard of true peace . . .
Keep us faithful to the ways of your commandments.

Loving Son, you challenge us with a new standard to live by.
Confront us with the consequences of our actions and lead us to
   repentance . . .
Restore in all people the image of your glory.

Loving Spirit, breathe upon your frail ones your life-restoring presence . . .
Raise us up to sing of your goodness and mercy.

Blessed Lord, you hold all souls in life.
Bring all the departed to the place of refreshment and peace . . .
Bring us to share in the life you give.

Year B

Sing to the Lord a new song
For he has done marvellous things.

God of love, your Spirit extends beyond all boundaries to encompass the
whole world.
Unite all who share your name as members of the same family of
faith . . .
May your Church be one as you are one.

God of love, your Spirit breaks restrictions of nationality, race and
language.
Unite all people as members of the same human family . . .
Strengthen all who foster and seek peace.

God of love, your Spirit calls us together as friends and neighbours.
Give us concern for the needs of all in our community . . .
Expand our compassion beyond personal networks and affiliations.

God of love, your Spirit draws us to abide in your love.
Hold in your embrace all who are ill or at the limits of their
endurance . . .
Complete within us all your joy.

God of love, your Spirit breathes life into your creation.
In your Son, give new life to all who have died . . .
Bring us through the waters of death to the life eternal.

Year C

Give thanks to the Lord
Rejoice and praise his name.

God of peace, when we are anxious keep our vision on your eternal
  Word.
Fill your Church with confidence in your praises . . .
Inspire those with oversight to equip your Church for its mission and
  ministry.

God of peace, you lead us into truth.
Give wisdom to all who lead and shape the course of nations . . .
Open our hearts to your justice.

God of peace, your blessing is never dispensed at the expense of others.
Give us the same generosity and self-restraint that all may rejoice . . .
May we build our communities on this capacity for kindness and
  responsibility.

God of peace, you invite us to wholeness and well-being.
Pour out your healing love . . .
Bring us to dance and rejoice in your favour.

God of peace, risen and ascended your Son declares your unrestrained
  love.
Consecrate the lives of your faithful servants departed in peace . . .
Accept us with them into your eternal city.

Ascension Day

—————◆—————

Years A, B and C

Shout to the Lord with a cry of joy
We will rejoice in your glory.

Risen, ascended, glorified Lord, we kneel before you in humble
   adoration and awe.
Rule in our hearts and be at the centre of your Church . . .
Fulfil in your Church your work of redemption.

Exalted Lord, at your ascension your disciples still didn't understand the
   nature of your Kingdom.
Expand the vision of all in leadership and government, to be subject to
   your just and gentle rule . . .
Enfold in your love all humanity as citizens of your Kingdom.

Lord Jesus Christ, your name is above every name.
Open our minds to understand the scriptures and persist with them
   where they are difficult . . .
Shape us to be witnesses of your hope and grace.

Lord of hope and consolation, look with compassion on the anguish of a
   troubled world.
Be our strength and comfort in times of adversity . . .
Bless us with your holiness and lift our eyes to behold your glory.

Jesus, risen, ascended and glorified for our salvation,
we lay our lives before you in faith and trust.
Raise with you all who have died . . .
Bring us to sing your praises through all the earth.

Easter 7

Year A

Let the righteous be glad
Sing praises to the Lord.

Heavenly Father, in your Son Jesus Christ you share your life with
    our life.
Unite your Church in this vitality that it may witness to your truth . . .
Keep hold of your Church and treasure those whom you call by
    name.

Heavenly Father, your Son expanded the narrow vision of his disciples.
Enlarge the scope of our concern to embrace people of all nations and
    races . . .
Keep us watchful against all that would devour the weak and vulnerable.

Heavenly Father, you give us grace to share your love with one
    another.
Bless our families and friends, those closest to us and unknown strangers
    whom to know would enrich us . . .
Enfold all people within your loving arms.

Heavenly Father, hear the cry of all who cast their anxiety on your
    loving care . . .
Restore and strengthen us in your service.

Heavenly Father, your glory unites earth and heaven.
Gather to yourself the faithful departed . . .
Grant eternal life to all children of your possession.

Year B

Be exalted, O God, above the heavens
Let your glory be over all the earth.

Holy Father, all creation belongs to you.
Sanctify your Church in the truth of your word . . .
Keep under your protection all who call on you.

Holy Father, you set us in the world while offering us true citizenship of
    your Kingdom.
Help us build on the values of your eternity . . .
Guide all with responsibility of government in the paths of your justice.

Holy Father, rooted and grounded in you we stand secure.
Be with all under pressure from the unscrupulous, and at risk of being
    led astray by distorted argument . . .
Give us strength to shun lies and perversions of truth.

Holy Father, we place our trust in you.
Uphold and sustain all who watch with heart-ache the degeneration of
    one they love . . .
Shine your light into our darkness and despair.

Holy Father, in your Son we receive everlasting life.
In this hope we commend to you all the departed . . .
Bring us at the last to rejoice with you.

Year C

Rejoice in the Lord you righteous
Give thanks to his holy name.

God Most High, you call your Church to proclaim the way of salvation
in your Son Jesus Christ.
Keep us rejoicing in this faith and delighting in your praise . . .
Come, Holy Spirit, fill your Church with your life and love.

God Most High, you send us to be agents of your Kingdom.
Transform our hopes and fears to declare your glory in all our dealings
with one another . . .
Come, Holy Spirit, fill our nation and all nations with your life and love.

God Most High, you draw us together from diverse backgrounds into a
commonwealth of your Son.
Deepen our respect and appreciation of your rainbow people . . .
Come, Holy Spirit, fill all people with your life and love.

God Most High, you heal our pain, bind up our wounds and restore us
for your glory.
Pour your blessing upon all whom we bring before you . . .
Come, Holy Spirit, fill us and all for whom we pray with your life and
love.

God Most High, you give to those who desire you a living spring
gushing up to eternal life.
Raise in your name all who have died . . .
Come, Holy Spirit, gather all the departed into the life and love of your
eternity.

Pentecost (Whit Sunday)

Year A

Send forth your Holy Spirit, O God
Renew the face of the earth.

Breathe on your Church, O God, your holy and life-giving Spirit.
Refresh and revive it with your vibrancy . . .
Pour out your gifts that your glory may be proclaimed throughout the
world.

Breathe on your creation, O God, your holy and life-giving Spirit.
Spread abroad from sea to sea and shore to shore your peace . . .
Your works will sing your praises.

Breathe on all flesh, O God, your holy and life-giving Spirit.
Unite into one family and fellowship the fragmented strands of
humanity . . .
Bring all people to rejoice in the wonders of your love.

Breathe on all who are frail and weary, O God, your holy and
life-giving Spirit . . .
Refresh them with the living waters that flow from you.

Breathe on all who have died, O God, your holy and life-restoring
Spirit . . .
May we all come to rejoice in your presence.

Year B

Pour out your Spirit, O Lord
We will rejoice in all your works.

Holy Spirit, come to your Church.
Refresh us in your truth and vision . . .
Give courage to all who call upon your name to testify to your saving
   love.

Holy Spirit, come to your world.
Unite disparate and diverse peoples . . .
Turn our sneering into wonder at your amazing deeds.

Holy Spirit, come to your creation.
Renew the face of the earth with your life-giving presence . . .
Cleanse and revive the product of your outpouring love.

Holy Spirit, come to your people.
Bring comfort to all in any kind of distress or weakness . . .
Restore us in your mercy.

Holy Spirit, come to your adopted children.
Bring to life all who hope in you . . .
Open to us the gates of paradise.

Year C

I will rejoice in the Lord
Your glory endures for ever.

Spirit of truth, come to your Church.
Fill us with love for the Father and the Son . . .
Guide us in holding to your commandments in essence and with integrity.

Spirit of truth, come to the nations.
Lead those who govern to build communities in which all may prosper . . .
Extend our horizons to embrace all people.

Spirit of truth, come to our relationships.
Move between us to strengthen the bonds which unite, and heal the
   wounds that divide . . .
Shape us to flourish as heirs of your grace.

Spirit of truth, come to all who are weary and carrying heavy burdens.
Set us free to praise you . . .
Refresh us all in your vibrant hope.

Spirit of truth, come to the darkness of death.
Make light to dawn for those whose hearts are weighed down with
   grief . . .
Bring to fulfilment salvation for all who call upon your name.

Trinity Sunday

Year A

Lord of life, truth and grace
Bring all creation to delight in your peace.

God of love, your mystery lies at the root of all creation.
Deepen our awareness of your awesome Being . . .
Everlasting God, we exalt your name in all the world.

Lord of grace, you reach through eternity to touch our mortal frame.
Set our limited concerns in the wider vision of your truth . . .
As you share our life, so may we come to share in your divine glory.

Holy Spirit of fellowship, move between us to unite all people in one
 community.
Strengthen all that builds cohesive living . . .
God of peace, be present in our midst.

Triune God, in your eternal vision you hold creation from its beginning
 to its end.
Sustain in your love all who are faint or whose strength is failing . . .
Restore our faith that you are with us to the end of the age.

Father, Son and Holy Spirit, you make us little lower than angels, and
 are mindful of all people.
With love and thanksgiving, we commend to you all who have died . . .
Adorn all the departed with your glory and honour.

Year B

Worship the Lord in the beauty of holiness
Let the whole earth rejoice.

Holy Lord, the earth is filled with your glory.
Purify our hearts and lives that we may hear your voice and call . . .
Send your Church to declare the mystery of your love.

Holy Lord, Nicodemus came by night seeking illumination and
    understanding.
Shine your light on the path of world leaders . . .
Give your people the blessing of peace.

Holy Lord, your Being is complete and yet you create us to share your
    life.
Expand our horizons to welcome strangers and friends . . .
Strengthen the bonds of our community.

Holy Lord, you bring healing and reconciliation.
Restore us in your image . . .
Give rest to the weary and hope to all who despair.

Holy Lord, your will is to save not condemn.
Look in mercy on all who have died . . .
Bring us to share the life of your eternity.

Year C

Lord of all
We exalt you in all the earth.

Holy and blessed Trinity, your love overflows to bring life and form to birth.
Set your Church on this dynamic foundation . . .
Fill us with your grace and truth.

Holy and blessed Trinity, within you is perfect unity.
Gather the nations, near and far, into one family . . .
Teach us to value the riches of this diverse family.

Holy and blessed Trinity, you break down barriers.
Give courage to risk encounters with strangers and enemies . . .
By your forgiveness, open the way to reconciliation where the path seems impossible.

Holy and blessed Trinity, between you there is mutual respect and care.
Hold in your triune grasp all who look for wholeness to be restored . . .
In all our sufferings deepen our hope in you.

Holy and blessed Trinity, all life is grounded in your Being.
Adorn with your glory and honour all who have died . . .
Bring us with them to your eternal peace.

Proper 3
(Between 24 and 28 May,
if after Trinity Sunday)

Years A, B and C

See pages 43 to 45 above.

Proper 4
(Between 29 May and 4 June,
if after Trinity Sunday)

———•◆•———

Year A

Lord of hosts
We put our trust in you.

God our rock, you are our sure foundation.
Keep your Church stable in the buffeting of the storms of this world . . .
Let us not be put to confusion.

God our rock, in your commandments we find the path of true peace.
Give courage to governments and councils to order common affairs with
    wisdom and decency . . .
Keep us from corruption and violence.

God our rock, in your embrace we grow in confidence and worth.
Give strength to those who provide the secure grounding for their
    families and communities . . .
May all homes provide the stability we need to flourish.

God our rock, you show the wonders of your love in a besieged city.
Be with all who feel exposed to turbulent and chaotic times . . .
In trouble and strife, may we know that you are God.

God our rock, there is nothing that can overcome your love for us.
Raise to new life all who have been overwhelmed by death . . .
In you is our salvation.

Year B

We will wait for the Lord
Our hope is in your word.

Lord of the Sabbath, your holiness bids us be still and adore.
As we marvel at all you have made may your Church display your life
and love . . .
Make us trusted advocates of your word.

Lord of the Sabbath, you set slaves free.
Raise up prophets to speak out for dignity and respect . . .
Disturb the complacent and open the eyes of all to your freedom.

Lord of the Sabbath, your compassion allows the hungry to be fed.
Challenge the hardness of our hearts when rules are blind to suffering
and oppression . . .
Give charity to open doors to your love and redemption.

Lord of the Sabbath, you bring healing and release from all that would
lock us in despair.
Reach out in your mercy to all who call upon you . . .
Anoint and cheer troubled minds with the abundance of your grace.

Lord of the Sabbath, you bring life and light to shine out of darkness.
Remember for good all who have died . . .
In Christ bring us to share in the glory of your Kingdom.

Year C

Sing to the Lord all the earth
Bless his holy name.

Lord, your command is sufficient to set us free yet you choose to come
among us.
Set your Church as a sign and embodiment of your living presence . . .
Make us worthy of your name which we bear.

Lord, as the centurion knew himself to be under authority,
keep all rulers mindful of the responsibility they carry . . .
Through devotion to your service preserve us from the corrosive effects
of power.

Lord, the centurion was honoured for providing a place for the
community to worship.
Bless all who commit to civic engagement and provide places for groups
to meet . . .
Enrich our belonging and strengthen all that fosters cohesive living.

Lord, the centurion placed trust in your healing power.
In our strength and weakness refresh our faith in your providential
care . . .
Put a new song in our hearts and on our lips.

Lord, we will declare your salvation from day to day.
Raise to your eternal glory all who have died . . .
Make us children and heirs of your redemption.

Proper 5
(Between 5 and 11 June,
if after Trinity Sunday)

***

Year A

Lord of hosts
We put our trust in you.

Lord, you found Matthew at the tax booth and called him to follow.
May your Church be as ready to respond to your summons . . .
Make us a blessing, not a curse.

Lord, Pharisees were shocked at your mercy.
Inspire our policies with your desire for redemption and repentance . . .
As your promise rests on grace, so may we order our common life
    towards your generosity.

Lord, our taxes contribute towards common services.
We pray for the work of tax officials and HM Treasury . . .
Challenge our selfish greed and make us wise stewards of your rich
    bounty.

Lord, you stopped to heal a woman blighted by years of suffering.
Show your compassion on all who are wearied by their ailments . . .
Bring wholeness and deep healing to all who reach out to you.

Lord, at your touch the little girl was restored to life.
Hear the cry of all whose hearts are torn by grief . . .
Bring us to rise with you.

Proper 5 (Between 5 and 11 June)

Year B

We will wait for the Lord
Our hope is in your Word.

Lord Jesus, crowds flocked to see you.
As we kneel before your presence, draw us together to become your
    body, the Church . . .
Give us thankful hearts with which to praise you.

Lord Jesus, some questioned your sanity and motives.
Stand alongside leaders and elected representatives as they grapple with
    the pace of change and shifting social landscapes . . .
Hold before us a vision of your Kingdom to guide us through the mist
    of uncertainty.

Lord Jesus, you said that a closed heart shuts out your forgiveness.
Confront our stubbornness with your grace and truth . . .
In humility and peace bring us to delight in you.

Lord Jesus, you call servants of your will not just friends but members of
    your family.
Look in compassion on your brothers and sisters in their need . . .
We place our trust in your mercy.

Lord Jesus, you prepare for your family an eternal weight of glory.
Bring into your eternal presence all who have died trusting in you . . .
Raise us to live with you for ever.

Year C

Sing to the Lord all the earth
Bless his holy name.

Lord of life, your touch breaks through taboos and fear to revive those
    held in the grip of death.
Breathe new life into your Church that we may dare to announce your
    freedom and peace . . .
Set free all who bear your name to proclaim your glory.

Lord of life, your grace turns violent hearts to righteousness and justice.
Transform in the light of your generous love our warring madness and
    fear . . .
Give to all leaders courage and compassion to promote your peace.

Lord of life, your purposes hold us all our days.
Bless our work that it may be fruitful and serve your Kingdom . . .
Keep from despair all who struggle to make ends meet.

Lord of life, your compassion reaches to the depths of our being.
Pour out your healing mercy on all who suffer . . .
Give us cause to sing your praises in sickness and in health.

Lord of life, your love turns our sorrow into dancing.
Hear the cry of all overcome by grief . . .
May we with all the departed hear you call us to rise.

Proper 6
(Between 12 and 18 June,
if after Trinity Sunday)

———◆———

Year A

Lord of hosts
We put our trust in you.

Lord of the harvest, send labourers for your Church to proclaim your
    Kingdom.
Stir up vocations to ordained and lay ministries . . .
Strengthen all the baptized to live and announce your glory.

Lord of all the world, inspire men and women to political service.
Transform unjust structures that all may have cause for rejoicing . . .
We give thanks for lives dedicated to the good of all.

Lord of hospitality, as Abraham welcomed strangers and received your
    blessing,
so we give thanks for all who share their table . . .
Bless the work of day centres and night shelters.

Lord, in proclaiming the Kingdom to have come near the sick were
    healed and good news announced for all.
Pour out your Spirit on all who are sick . . .
Restore us to wholeness with you.

Lord of life, you prove your love for us in your death and resurrection.
Open the gates of heaven to all who believe in you . . .
Grant to all your faithful servants eternal peace.

Year B

We will wait for the Lord
Our hope is in your Word.

Lord, your love urges us on.
Give your Church confidence to trust in your new creation . . .
Bring to fulfilment the promises of your Kingdom.

Lord, your love sits in judgement over our deeds whether good or
  evil.
Search the hearts of all and inspire the course of justice and concord . . .
We will trust in your name.

Lord, your love grows within us as a seed germinates in the ground.
Bring to full bloom the flowering of your grace . . .
May we all delight in the shade and protection of your favour.

Lord, your love holds us through all trials and tribulations.
Look in compassion on all who cry for relief in their suffering . . .
Grant that we may tell of your loving-kindness all the day long.

Lord, your love raised Jesus from the dead for our salvation.
As our old nature passes away, bring us into your new order . . .
Remember us in your Kingdom of mercy.

Year C

Sing to the Lord all the earth
Bless his holy name.

Lord of grace and mercy, your love penetrates into the depths of our
hearts.
Give to your Church this charitable judgement, that all may find release
from the bondage of sin . . .
May we proclaim and bring the good news of your Kingdom.

Lord of grace and mercy, you invite leaders and rulers to discern the
path of liberation.
Transform our politics with your justice and wisdom . . .
Save us from easy divisions that obscure your truth and glory.

Lord of grace and mercy, you give freely of your bounty,
and yet some go hungry while others are overfed.
Set free all locked into the spiral of debt and poverty . . .
All are welcome at the table of your Kingdom.

Lord of grace and mercy, you bring healing to troubled hearts and
minds.
Pour out the oil of your salvation on all anxious in their frailty . . .
Raise up all laid low in despair and fear.

Lord of grace and mercy, you honour the people of your promise.
Draw all who have died in your faith to your eternity . . .
We will rejoice and be glad in you.

Proper 7
(Between 19 and 25 June,
if after Trinity Sunday)

Year A

Lord of hosts
We put our trust in you.

Lord Jesus, your light penetrates the secrets of our hearts.
Be at the centre of your Church, that we may love you above
    everything else . . .
Give us grace to walk in newness of life.

Lord Jesus, your love exposes both deeds of darkness and light.
Drive away the fear that oppresses and demeans . . .
Give courage to those in authority to defend and uphold the good
    of all.

Lord Jesus, you hold everyone precious in your sight.
Look with compassion on all who are marginalized and rejected . . .
Raise up all who suffer reproach and shame for your sake.

Lord Jesus, you show great love towards all who call upon you.
Keep watch over them . . .
Gladden the hearts of your servants in their need.

Lord Jesus, raised from the dead you die no more.
Hear us as we remember in this faith and love those who have died . . .
As you break the hold of death so may we come to share your life in
    glory.

Year B

We will wait for the Lord
Our hope is in your Word.

Lord, your disciples cried to you in distress.
Hear your Church when faith falters and the waves threaten to
    overwhelm . . .
Still the clamour of anxious doubts.

Lord, your ancient people feared destruction when faced by Goliath.
Give wisdom and imagination to leaders as they face challenges that look
    unbeatable . . .
Deliver us from all evil.

Lord, you chose fishermen to be among your closest companions.
Be with all who sail the seas . . .
Bless the work of the RNLI and all who go to those in distress.

Lord, when the wind blows and the storm gathers, speak your words of
    peace.
Breathe into our despairing your calm and tranquil presence . . .
Give rest to the weary and hope to all who suffer.

Lord, there is no disaster that you cannot redeem.
Give life to all over whom the waters of death have closed . . .
Bring us to rejoice in your salvation.

Year C

Sing to the Lord all the earth
Bless his holy name.

Most High God, all creation knows you and is alive with your presence.
Join our worship with the natural praises of all you have made . . .
With humble and contrite hearts we adore your name.

Most High God, your authority is over all.
Give governments and rulers wisdom for the awesome responsibility they
    bear . . .
As fellow heirs of your promise, remove all false barriers and distinctions
    between people.

Most High God, you test the hearts of your people.
Be with all facing examinations on which their futures depend . . .
Give us grace to value the diversity of gifts and talents you give.

Most High God, your compassion sees beyond fear.
Hold with your mercy all whose mental state is diminished or
    damaged . . .
Embrace them in your love that we may yet give you thanks.

Most High God, you reveal yourself in the depth of sheer silence.
Teach us to know you and trust in your eternity as with faith we
    remember those who have died . . .
Bring us with them to rejoice in the fulfilment of your promise.

Proper 8
(Between 26 June and 2 July)

————◆◆◆————

Year A

I give thanks to you, O Lord, with my whole heart
I will glorify your name for ever.

Generous God, your love bids us welcome.
Give to your Church an open heart . . .
Unite your gathered people into a true fellowship of your Son.

Generous God, your Son gave a model of simple charity.
Transform our governance with such willing compassion . . .
May the hungry find food shared and the thirsty be revived.

Generous God, break down the barriers that divide communities and
 increase hostilities.
Extend the hands of friendship to soften hardened hearts . . .
Remove all that diminishes people's worth.

Generous God, pour out your love and compassion on all who cry
 'How long, O Lord' . . .
Shine your light into the darkness.

Generous God, receive with mercy and forgiveness all who have
 died . . .
Comfort those who grieve and bring us to share in the reward of the
 righteous.

Year B

It is good to give thanks to the Lord
We will sing praises to our God.

Lord of life, you raised Jairus' daughter from the clutches of death.
Fill your Church with new life to proclaim your wonders . . .
Remove the fear that blocks trust in you.

Lord of life, the leader Jairus begged for your help.
Be with all who carry the burden of government . . .
Turn our longing into zeal for your Kingdom.

Lord of life, your generosity brings riches beyond measure.
Expand the horizons of all responsible for financial planning . . .
Increase social capital and make us mindful of the consequence for
    all.

Lord of life, some cry out for your healing touch in secret and shame.
Pour out your compassion on all who are embarrassed at their
    condition . . .
Restore the dignity and self-worth of all who come to you.

Lord of life, you stretched out your hand and restored the little girl to life.
Hear the cries of all who mourn and long for what cannot be . . .
Turn our wailing into dancing at the promise of your resurrection.

Year C

Sing to the Lord a new song
Sing to the Lord, all the earth.

Lord, you rebuked your disciples for their hardness of heart and set high
    standards for those who would follow you.
Inspire in your Church the devotion and dedication required to be
    counted as your people . . .
We commit ourselves wholeheartedly to your will.

Lord, you set your face towards Jerusalem causing offence in some.
Take away all prejudice and foolish pride . . .
Give to leaders openness to work with everyone of goodwill.

Lord, your Spirit refreshes and enlivens our senses.
Keep us wholesome in our desires and faithful to your purposes . . .
Fill us with your gracious presence and loving-kindness in all things.

Lord, you know our fear and hold us in all adversity.
Be with all who care for loved ones and friends;
for those with dementia and reduced autonomy . . .
Hear our cry and be merciful to your children in their distress.

Lord, you give life and in your mercy new life to those who trust in
    you.
Deal tenderly with all who mourn . . .
When our time on earth is over, gather us with all your saints to be
    with you for ever.

Proper 9
(Between 3 and 9 July)

Year A

I give thanks to you, O Lord, with my whole heart
I will glorify your name for ever.

Gentle Lord Jesus, you are humble in heart and true security is found in
   your service.
Bring to your Church space to breathe amid turmoil and clamour . . .
Hush the voices of discord and loathing.

Gentle Lord Jesus, some sought to distort and attack you whatever you
   said or did.
Vindicate wise counsel and further the cause of justice and truth . . .
Give us strength that we may know and do what is right.

Gentle Lord Jesus, you give us grace to share your love and we delight
   in its warmth.
Bless parents and all who influence the young . . .
Enrich us with the fun, laughter and playfulness of youth.

Gentle Lord Jesus, you called the weary to come to you.
We lay at your feet our heavy burdens . . .
Recreate us in your love and devotion.

Gentle Lord Jesus, you bring life out of death and hope out of despair.
Turn our sorrow into dancing and our mourning into song . . .
Restore in your image and glory all who have entered into your rest.

Year B

It is good to give thanks to the Lord
We will sing praises to our God.

God of grace, you fill your Church with diverse gifts.
Inspire all who teach and expound the scriptures . . .
Fill us with a vision of your glory.

God of grace, you raised up great leaders from among your people.
Give to all in authority the wisdom and strength they need to match the
    hour . . .
Direct all nations in the paths of righteousness and truth.

God of grace, the Twelve were sent out relying on hospitality to sustain
    them.
Open the hearts of all to share of your bountiful goodness . . .
Make our communities places of welcome and care.

God of grace, the Twelve were sent to anoint the sick.
Pour out your healing Spirit on all in need . . .
In our weakness may the power of your Christ dwell within us.

God of grace, Jesus knew the love of family and friends.
Be with all who mourn the loss of someone close . . .
We entrust all who have died into the hope of your life and love.

Year C

Sing to the Lord a new song
Sing to the Lord, all the earth.

Lord, you bid us proclaim peace and announce your Kingdom.
Strengthen your Church for this ministry in your name . . .
Send labourers with the necessary gifts to gather people to worship and
    grow in your grace.

Lord, you invite your followers to sit light to material possessions.
Turn us from perpetual grasping for wealth and status . . .
Give to all who guide the state wisdom to shape the common good after
    your justice.

Lord, you declared that workers deserve fair pay for their labours.
May all find an outlet for their gifts and contribute to the well-being of
    society . . .
Give courage to all who strive for fair conditions of employment.

Lord, you sent out disciples to cure the sick.
Bind up our wounds of body and mind . . .
Give hope in suffering and bring us all to rejoice in your rich bounty.

Lord, your love extends beyond length of days.
Reach into the depths of our sorrow and raise us to the brightness of
    your new day . . .
Restore life where it has been lost and bring us to the joy of your
    eternal Kingdom.

Proper 10
(Between 10 and 16 July)

———•◆•———

Year A

I give thanks to you, O Lord, with my whole heart
I will glorify your name for ever.

God of wisdom and understanding,
be with your Church as we seek to understand your purpose and will.
Nurture and tend all new to faith . . .
By your Holy Spirit, bring to fruition the seed of your word.

God of endurance and reliability,
be with your world obsessed by many cares and short-term gains.
Renew the face of the earth . . .
By your Holy Spirit, inspire all people to sustainable living.

God of seedtime and harvest, be with all who tend and manage the land;
for food to nourish and spaces for recreation . . .
By your Holy Spirit, open our hearts to share the fruits of the field in
    their seasons.

God of hope and consolation, deal tenderly with all for whom life is full
    of struggle.
Give them strength and patience in their sufferings . . .
By your Holy Spirit, bring us to rejoice in your presence.

God of life and peace, you set your creation in motion.
Bring to fulfilment the purpose you set for each one of us . . .
By your Holy Spirit, bring us to dwell with you for ever.

Year B

It is good to give thanks to the Lord
We will sing praises to our God.

King of glory, your prophets sought to restore your people to be true
  and sure.
Set your Church on the firm foundation of your Son . . .
Bless us with the riches of your grace.

King of glory, Herod abused his position.
Keep us from contempt for your ways and your people . . .
Strengthen all who speak bravely for justice and honesty.

King of glory, you excite our hearts with music and dancing.
Fill us with joy at the life you give . . .
Increase within us thankfulness for the creative arts.

King of glory, in your passion you lift our human frailty to your divine
  glory.
Give hope to all who endure great suffering or whose endurance is
  breaking . . .
Strengthen and sustain all who are weighed down.

King of glory, John's disciples came to bury his body with dignity and
  love.
Be alongside those who weep or mourn . . .
Bring us all to share in the inheritance of your redemption.

Year C

Sing to the Lord a new song
Sing to the Lord, all the earth.

God of mercy, you teach us that faith without works of charity and
compassion is dead.
Give to your Church a heart for service . . .
May the good news we proclaim be shown in word and deed.

God of mercy, you show us that no one is above caring for neighbours
in need.
Stir the hearts of those with means to use their wealth for the good of
all . . .
Give us a generous will to contribute to the common good.

God of mercy, you draw us from isolation into communities of love and
support.
Give us grace to befriend the lonely, support the struggling and guide
the young . . .
Forgive us the occasions when we pass by on the other side deliberately
and unintentionally, or when services are overwhelmed.

God of mercy, you are near to us and sustain us in whatever adversity
we face.
Shine the light of your presence upon all who suffer . . .
Give hope and peace to troubled hearts.

God of mercy, with you is the well of life.
Remember for good all who have died . . .
Gather all the departed in gentleness and peace to the safety of your
eternal Kingdom.

Proper 11
(Between 17 and 23 July)

Year A

I give thanks to you, O Lord, with my whole heart
I will glorify your name for ever.

Righteous Father, through your Son we are adopted as heirs of your
    glory.
Keep your Church faithful to this hope . . .
Open our hearts to be receptive to your awesome presence.

Righteous Father, give to governments due proportion in guarding and
    protecting their people from those of evil intent . . .
Turn all our hearts from ways of hatred to peace.

Righteous Father, your love shows compassion and restraint to children
    of your Kingdom and to those who would disrupt it.
Give us the same patience and grace to be agents of your transforming
    love . . .
Fortify us in the struggle of your dawning Kingdom.

Righteous Father, as we wait with longing for your glory,
be with all who groan and endure hardship . . .
Bring your light to our darkness.

Righteous Father, gather to yourself all whose earthly days have come to
    an end . . .
May they shine in the brightness of your eternal glory.

Year B

It is good to give thanks to the Lord
We will sing praises to our God.

Jesus, true shepherd of your people, you gathered your apostles round
you.
Draw your Church close to you as it seeks to proclaim your name in the
world . . .
Refresh us in your life and love.

Jesus, true shepherd of your people, you break down the divisions of
birth and creed.
Unite all people under the covenant of your grace . . .
May all hear peace announced to them.

Jesus, true shepherd of your people, give rest to the weary and all whose
work brings them to the point of exhaustion . . .
We give thanks for places of renewal and re-creation.

Jesus, true shepherd of your people,
look with compassion on all desperate for your healing touch . . .
Restore us in the promise of your Kingdom.

Jesus, true shepherd of your people,
we lay before you all who have died . . .
As you make us a dwelling place for you, so may we come to dwell
with you for ever.

Year C

Sing to the Lord a new song
Sing to the Lord, all the earth.

Christ our hope of glory, still our clamouring hearts,
that we may sit with devotion in your presence.
Give your Church faith to sing of your majesty . . .
May our action never become a substitute for being at one with you.

Christ our hope of glory, give to all leaders and rulers space to reflect on
    your will.
Come to them in the quiet and breathing spaces squeezed into busy
    diaries . . .
Restore a right vision and sense of priorities.

Christ our hope of glory, in hospitality some have entertained angels and
    met with you.
Open our hearts to share our food with friends and strangers in need . . .
Bless soup kitchens and lunch clubs and everywhere that bread is broken
    and shared.

Christ our hope of glory, in our suffering we share in your passion.
Strengthen all who call out to you in distress . . .
Give us such depth of joy that we may rejoice in you.

Christ our hope of glory, you hold before us the promise of salvation.
Deliver us at the hour of our death . . .
Bring us to that banquet where saints and angels delight in your eternal
    presence.

Proper 12
(Between 24 and 30 July)

———•◆•———

Year A

I give thanks to you, O Lord, with my whole heart
I will glorify your name for ever.

Lord, your Kingdom as a mustard seed grows through small devotions.
Take from us our inflated pride that we may regard with awe and
    wonder the small signs of its birth . . .
Grow your Church into a place where all may find a spiritual
    home.

Lord, your Kingdom like yeast in dough permeates through all the
    world.
Inspire men and women to make a difference through their political
    service . . .
Pour out your transforming love.

Lord, your Kingdom like treasure in a field excites our hearts at its
    discovery.
Give us grace to share the blessings received, so advancing their value
    and worth for all . . .
Your gifts enrich us beyond measure.

Lord, your Kingdom, like a pearl of great price, is our true heart's desire.
Fill the hearts of all who suffer with this delight in your goodness . . .
We will sing your praises and glory in your name, O Lord.

Lord, your Kingdom is like a net hauling in a great catch.
Bring us and all who have died into the safety of your eternity . . .
At the end may your holy angels lead us to paradise.

Year B

It is good to give thanks to the Lord
We will sing praises to our God.

Lord, your love surpasses all understanding.
Fill your Church with your bountiful Spirit
that it may make known your glory . . .
We will rejoice and sing your praises.

Lord, your justice confronts the scheming and plotting of violence and
   corruption.
Transform our politics to serve your will and advance your peace . . .
Help us to see through the storms of our fear to the land of promise you
   hold out before us.

Lord, your provision exceeds our need and we share in your rich
   bounty.
Give us grace to display the same generosity and thanksgiving in how we
   share the fruits of blessing . . .
Unite us as members of your family.

Lord, your foresight reaches out to our desires before we have
   approached you.
Stretch out your hands to bless all who long for healing and release from
   their sufferings . . .
Grant that we may find a voice to praise you for your mercy and
   goodness.

Lord, your life holds us through the darkness of death and grief.
Bring to fulfilment the promise of your glory . . .
Deliver us from death to life.

Year C

Sing to the Lord a new song
Sing to the Lord, all the earth.

Heavenly Father, we praise your name.
As you pour out your Holy Spirit upon your Church, so may we labour
as midwives of your Kingdom . . .
Build your Church and root it in your Son.

Heavenly Father, you set us in a garden of promise and fruitfulness.
Give us the will to share your bounty with fairness, ensuring all are
fed . . .
Guide the nations in justice and peace.

Heavenly Father, you set aside our sin and release us from its bonds.
Bring your liberty to all enslaved by tyranny and exploitation . . .
Raise up prophets and champions of the weak and vulnerable.

Heavenly Father, you are always ready to hear the cry of those who call
out to you.
In your mercy pour out your blessing on all who suffer . . .
Fill our hearts with joy and gladness.

Heavenly Father, our life is bound up with your life.
Hold us all our days and bring us at the last to your eternal city . . .
Grant to all the inheritance prepared for your beloved children.

Proper 13
(Between 31 July and 6 August)

Year A

Give thanks to the Lord
Call upon his name.

Jesus, living bread, we come to this meal as your guests.
Unite all whom you invite into a closer body . . .
Forgive and heal the divisions of our making.

Jesus, living bread, you ensure none go hungry from your banquet.
Stir leaders and governments to change structures that impoverish and
    lead to destitution . . .
Forgive and overturn injustice whatever form it takes.

Jesus, living bread, crowds came out to you.
Be among those who gather for festivals, summer camps and celebrations
    of your Word . . .
Refresh in us zeal for your gospel.

Jesus, living bread, your healing touch reached out to the sick.
Pour out your restoring presence on all who call out to you . . .
Lift up all who are bowed down.

Jesus, living bread, you mourned the death of John the Baptist.
Look with compassion on all who mourn . . .
Raise us to new life with you.

Year B

Sing praises to the Lord
Whose love endures for ever.

Jesus, bread of life, feed your Church with your gifts of faith and trust.
Equip us for the ministry to which you call all baptized in your
name . . .
Grant that we may grow into maturity in union with you.

Jesus, bread of life, nourish our public life with your gift of prophetic
wisdom.
Inspire us to look beyond immediate needs and shallow pleasures . . .
Grant that all may delight in your goodness.

Jesus, bread of life, sustain our life with your gift of sufficient food and
water.
Give us the will to ensure none go hungry or are malnourished . . .
Bless the work of aid agencies and trade justice movements.

Jesus, bread of life, revive all who are weary and exhausted with your
gift of patient hope.
Strengthen and uphold them in their sufferings . . .
Refresh them with knowledge of your presence.

Jesus, bread of life, restore us in the gift of your eternal life.
Hear our prayer as we remember those who have died . . .
Grant us to share with them in the eternal banquet of your love.

Year C

God, our joy and strength
We will sing of your glory.

Generous God, your love sets us free and fills us with your grace.
Set our hearts at peace that we may trust in your rich bounty . . .
Give us patient and pure hearts, O God.

Generous God, we pray for all troubled by their economic state:
for farmers anxious about their crops;
for traders anxious about market fluctuations;
for those who feel shut out from access to wealth and sufficient for the
    day . . .
In all things teach us to celebrate the gifts of your abundant love.

Generous God, you unite us in a common wealth.
We pray for our community . . .
Bind us together and expand our charity to reach all your people.

Generous God, your compassion extends throughout creation.
Hear our prayer for all in any kind of need . . .
Sustain them in their troubles and restore in them hope in you.

Generous God, you are the source and goal of all life.
We lay before your love all who have died . . .
At the final judgement draw us all to your treasury in heaven.

Proper 14
(Between 7 and 13 August)

———◆———

Year A

Give thanks to the Lord
Call upon his name.

Lord, it is you who comes when we cry out in storm-tossed moments.
Reach out to your Church when sight of the strong wind brings
    fear . . .
Open our ears to hear you say 'take heart'.

Lord, it is you who sends your disciples to cross the lake.
Be with all who travel by land, sea and air for holidays, business and
    missions of mercy . . .
Direct those who guard our safety.

Lord, it is you who went up the mountain to pray alone.
Come to us in the still moments to refresh, revive and reignite the fire
    of living . . .
Increase in us thanksgiving for your saving mercy.

Lord, it is you who reaches out to us when we cry 'Lord save me'.
Catch all who are falling in their frailty . . .
Everyone who calls on the name of the Lord shall be saved.

Lord, it is you who appears in the early morning on the water and later
    in the garden.
Bring all who have died to delight in the sound of your voice . . .
With the whole host of heaven we worship your holy name.

Year B

Sing praises to the Lord
Whose love endures for ever.

Heavenly Father, in your love draw us deeper into your presence.
Give to your Church grace to imitate your Son . . .
Nourish us with the food that leads to eternal life.

Heavenly Father, calm our words that we may use them to build up and
    nurture in your way.
Put away from us the ways of malice and evil . . .
Sustain those who lead in pursuing justice and peace.

Heavenly Father, when the going is hard save us from despair and
    faltering.
Put behind your people the complaining that saps strength and joy . . .
Renew within us a song of thanksgiving and praise.

Heavenly Father, prevent the angry being consumed by hatred and
    bitterness.
Strengthen the weak and weary . . .
In your tender love, restore your people.

Heavenly Father, you have marked your children with the seal of
    redemption.
Hear our prayer for all who have died . . .
May we pass through death to life with you for ever.

Year C

God our joy and strength
We will sing of your glory.

Faithful God, we wait on your Word and our hearts rejoice in your
  loving-kindness.
Renew our confidence in the promise of your Kingdom and the signs of
  its dawning . . .
Keep your Church vigilant and expectant.

Faithful God, set our hearts on the lasting treasure of your Son.
Keep us from the complacency that is blind to injustice . . .
Extend our concern to new horizons.

Faithful God, we pray for all who share our spiritual ancestry:
especially Muslims and Jews, fellow sons and daughters of Abraham . . .
We pray for a greater understanding between our faiths;
for all that builds and sustains cohesive living.

Faithful God, strengthen all who are fearful of the future;
all going through a vale of misery . . .
Strengthen the faint-hearted, support the weak and raise up the broken-
  hearted.

Faithful God, prepare us for the day when we will come to share in
  your eternal banquet.
We commend to you those who have died in this hope . . .
Welcome us home to the celestial city you have made ready for your
  beloved children.

Proper 15
(Between 14 and 20 August)

Year A

Give thanks to the Lord
Call upon his name.

God of purity, cleanse our thoughts of all that would abuse or demean
others.
Forgive the sins we do and those we dream that infect our character . . .
With heart and mind and voice we will sing your praises.

God of compassion, your Son had his scope expanded by the Canaanite
woman's persistence.
Challenge the boundaries we set to our charity and concern . . .
May your justice give cause for all to delight in you.

God of hospitality, you set a place for all at your table.
Open our hearts to embrace those easily excluded and despised . . .
We will declare your saving health among all peoples.

God of healing, at your word the girl was released from her distress.
Announce your freedom to all weighed down with sickness and
infirmity . . .
Lord, have mercy on all in their distress.

God of hope, you bring life to all who call upon your name.
Draw into your eternal family all who have died . . .
Restore the fortunes of your people, O Lord.

142

Year B

Sing praises to the Lord
Whose love endures for ever.

Lord, in your love you enable us to share in your life.
So fill your Church with this vitality that it may proclaim your glory to
all the world . . .
As we share in the sacrament of your body and blood, may we abide in
you as you abide in us.

Lord, in your love you pour out your gift of wisdom.
Give to those with responsibility for government a wise and discerning
mind . . .
Grant that all nations may walk with insight and truth.

Lord, in your love you set before us a model of wholesome living.
Keep us from false substitutes for true spiritual and emotional health . . .
Set free all bound by alcohol or drug dependency.

Lord, in your love you regard the weak and vulnerable.
Send your Spirit upon all hungry for your healing touch . . .
At all times and in everything, teach us to sing your praises.

Lord, in your love you hold out to us the promise of eternal life.
Remember for good all who have died . . .
As we feed on you, so may we come to share in your life for ever.

Year C

God our joy and strength
We will sing of your glory.

Lord of time and eternity, you call your Church to prophetic voice.
Inspire all who bear your name to persevere in seeking your will . . .
May the vineyard of our lives bear fruit in the warmth of your love.

Lord of time and eternity, you judge us with mercy and truth.
Hear the cry of all who long for justice:
the poor and weak; all at the mercy of the unscrupulous and violent . . .
Give us courage to choose life in all its fullness.

Lord of time and eternity, we pray for all whose stance brings them into
conflict . . .
Give us humble and contrite hearts,
standing for whatever is honourable and noble
and building bridges where reconciliation may grow.

Lord of time and eternity, you are tender and gentle with all who are
afflicted.
Show compassion on all who seek your healing touch . . .
Restore us, O Lord, in the light of your countenance.

Lord of time and eternity, you came to save the lost and restore the
fallen.
In your mercy, gather to yourself those who have died . . .
Raise us with them to share in the bounty of your love.

Proper 16
(Between 21 and 27 August)

———•◆•———

Year A

Give thanks to the Lord
Call upon his name.

Son of Man, you build your Church on both the strength and frailty of
    your disciples.
Pour out the riches of your grace,
that with diverse gifts your Church may further your Kingdom . . .
Nothing shall prevail against your will.

Son of Man, before you nations are humbled.
Remove the fear that leads to oppression and contempt that diminishes
    human worth . . .
Strengthen all that leads to cohesive living.

Son of Man, you bring to birth hope and new life.
Bless all who work in maternity services and care for the newborn . . .
Wrap all life in your tender love.

Son of Man, you fulfil the hopes and dreams of all ages.
Be with all who long for relief from their suffering . . .
Anoint us with your Holy Spirit.

Son of Man, your glory is revealed in your death and resurrection.
We entrust to you all who have died . . .
Unlock the gates of paradise that all may enter in.

145

Year B

Sing praises to the Lord
Whose love endures for ever.

Jesus, Holy One, you are the Word of eternal life.
Strengthen and encourage your Church in declaring your love . . .
Keep us faithful however difficult is the message we proclaim.

Jesus, Holy One, surround with your spiritual armour all who defend the
    vulnerable and powerless.
Give courage to leaders to advance the cause of all with equity . . .
Sustain the integrity of those under pressure where conflict or selfishness
    would triumph.

Jesus, Holy One, you knew the companionship of friends and the pain
    of people turning away.
Be with the lonely and those who have been abandoned . . .
May we be secure in your love and affirmation.

Jesus, Holy One, speak your words of peace to any whose mind is
    troubled.
Bless us all whatever our distress . . .
Open your ears to our cry.

Jesus, Holy One, be near to the broken-hearted.
Raise up those who have died . . .
Grant that we may dwell in your house for ever.

Year C

God our joy and strength
We will sing of your glory.

Holy God,
you refuse to be bound by any constraints our limited vision would seek
to impose.
Transform the poverty of our faith by the riches of your grace . . .
May your Church be an instrument of blessing and release.

Holy God,
we pray for all who take counsel for nations:
for governments and councils, for all whose decisions affect the lives of
others . . .
May justice and righteousness prosper.

Holy God,
you refresh the face of the earth and your people.
Pour out your Spirit on all in need of renewal and Sabbath rest . . .
Restore us in your loving mercy.

Holy God, you know us from before our birth and hold us through all
our days.
Be with all whose spirits are weak and who seek to be set free from
their ailments . . .
Bring us to rejoice in the wonders of your healing touch.

Holy God,
you judge the hearts of all with truth and mercy.
Look with compassion on those who have died . . .
May our praise be always of you and our hope in your saving love.

Proper 17
(Between 28 August and 3 September)

Year A

Lord of faith and truth
We bless your holy name.

Lord Jesus, you shocked your disciples by making them face up to your
cross and their own.
Give to your Church courage to emulate your sacrificial love . . .
May we find our true life in you.

Lord Jesus, you spoke of suffering at the hands of elders and community
leaders.
Give to all who lead due awareness of the awesome responsibility they
hold . . .
May we never confuse kingdoms of this world with your eternal
Kingdom.

Lord Jesus, Peter struggled to accept the danger and purpose of your
actions.
Be with all who are anxious for a loved one whose job places them in
grave danger . . .
Give us grace to overcome evil with good.

Lord Jesus, you are with us as we stand staring into the darkness.
Preserve us in all our sufferings . . .
Grant us compassion to rejoice with those who rejoice and weep with
those who weep.

Lord Jesus, you hold open the door to eternity.
Strengthen all who stand on its threshold in faith and fear . . .
We will rejoice in your hope.

Year B

We call upon your name, O Lord
Incline your ear to our prayer.

God of purity, you see into the depths of our hearts.
Keep your Church from the corruption of evil intent . . .
As we honour your name so may we live to your praise.

God of purity, you see our scheming and political intrigue.
Keep the nations from oppression and violence . . .
May nothing take precedence over respect for life.

God of purity, you see our desires and emotional blindness.
Keep us from covetousness and deception . . .
May fidelity and self-restraint be treasured and prevail.

God of purity, you see the pains of the world whether public or secret.
Keep your people from despair and despondency . . .
May all who call on you know the consolation of your love.

God of purity, you see the sorrow and distress of all who grieve.
Keep hold of your beloved at the hour of our death . . .
May we rise with you in glory.

Year C

God of abiding mercy
We will rejoice in you.

Generous God, you draw us deeper into your love and our hearts
    resound in your praise.
Fill your Church with your bountiful goodness,
that we may reach out to touch those beyond our usual gaze . . .
Make us hospitable, welcoming all as if your Son.

Generous God, you exalt those regarded as lowly, and humble those
    used to worldly honour.
Save all in high office from becoming contemptuous of the people they
    serve . . .
Train us in the humility that respects and furthers the common good.

Generous God, you share your bread with sinners and pilgrims equally,
that all may grow in the likeness of your Son.
We pray for all with whom we share in this banquet of your grace . . .
Increase the bonds that unite us in your fellowship.

Generous God, you promise that you will never forsake your people.
Be with all who feel shrouded in darkness or fear:
all anxious about what the future will hold, whose illness brings them
    close to despair . . .
May your light shine in the dark places.

Generous God, we praise and bless you for your eternal mercy.
In this faith we remember with love all who have died . . .
May we all come to hear you invite us into your nearer presence.

Proper 18
(Between 4 and 10 September)

Year A

Lord of faith and truth
We bless your holy name.

Lord, you are among us even when we are few in number gathered in
    your name.
Strengthen and bless all who meet to celebrate your sacraments and feed
    on your word . . .
In your love, fulfil all that your law upholds.

Lord, you are among us in disputes and agreements.
Open our hearts to your reconciling grace . . .
Heal the hurts of injuries borne and evil intent.

Lord, you are among us when we share food and tell our stories of your
    guiding presence.
Encourage and sustain us in your fellowship . . .
Come alongside us as we accompany one another on our journey of
    faith.

Lord, you are among us in sickness and health.
Teach us to see through our frailty to your loving mercy that always
    holds us . . .
For clinicians' skill and friends who are there whatever befalls, we give
    you thanks.

Lord, you are among us when tears flow and day turns to night.
Gather to yourself all who have died . . .
Bring us to the joy of the dawning new day of your resurrection.

Year B

We call upon your name, O Lord
Incline your ear to our prayer.

Open our ears, O Lord, to hear your call.
Release our tongues to proclaim your praises . . .
Give to your Church clear speech in announcing your gospel.

Open the ears of the nations, O Lord, to the cry for justice.
Release all oppressed and enslaved . . .
Give courage to all who announce your Kingdom.

Open our ears, O Lord, to the necessity for equality.
Release all demeaned by prejudice and discrimination . . .
Give perseverance to all who strive to remove bias and intolerance.

Open your ears, O Lord, to songs of suffering and distress.
Release all held in chains by debilitating diseases and pain . . .
Give hope to all who trust in you.

Open your ears, O Lord, to songs of lament and grief.
Release from the clutches of death all who have died . . .
Give grace to all who mourn to let go into the new life you bring.

Year C

God of abiding mercy
We will rejoice in you.

Lord Jesus,
you gave everything of yourself for our sake and yet our response can be
  so meagre.
Confront us with the challenge of your good news,
that we may give freely of all that we are and have in your service . . .
Refresh our hearts in you and fit us for your Kingdom.

Lord Jesus,
you break the false bonds we use to oppress and subjugate those you
  make free.
We pray for all who are set over others: managers and leaders . . .
Teach us that authority brings responsibility and that all power is
  ultimately yours.

Lord Jesus,
we give thanks for friends who support and minister to us in our hour
  of need;
for the service freely given and received . . .
Give us thankful hearts for the love expressed.

Lord Jesus,
you told your disciples to take up their cross in order to follow you.
Hear our prayer for all who find this hard to bear . . .
Teach us to trust in your providential care.

Lord Jesus,
your love moulds and shapes us for eternity with you.
We hold before you all whose earthly travail is over . . .
Bring us with them to delight in your nearer presence.

Proper 19
(Between 11 and 17 September)

Year A

Lord of faith and truth
We bless your holy name.

God of mercy, your love overwhelms us with your generous forgiveness.
Open our hearts to extend this charity to all who are penitent . . .
May your Church be a place where deliverance abounds.

God of mercy, you hold before us a model of justice tempered by
  mercy.
Inspire those in political office to promote the restoration of those who
  offend . . .
Bless the work of rehabilitation centres and projects.

God of mercy, you release us from a debt we can never repay.
We pray for all out of their depth financially and exposed to the
  unscrupulous . . .
Bless the work of credit unions and banks that promote responsible
  lending.

God of mercy, your compassion challenges us to work for relief from
  suffering.
Pour out your healing presence on all who struggle to cope with their
  illness . . .
Stand between us and all that would destroy us.

God of mercy, whether we live or die we are yours.
Receive in your love all who have died . . .
Bring us to the place where sins are cancelled and we dwell in the
equity of your love.

Year B

We call upon your name, O Lord
Incline your ear to our prayer.

Lord, you set your cross before us as the pathway to salvation.
Give your Church courage to embrace sacrificial living . . .
May we never be ashamed to proclaim you as Lord.

Lord, you set your cross before all nations as a challenge to power and
force.
Give courage to all who stand for justice and peace . . .
May all who govern serve their people with wisdom and humility.

Lord, you set your cross before all people as a sign of truth and
understanding.
Bless and guide all who teach and inspire the minds of the young . . .
May we set their feet on firm foundations for godly and fruitful lives.

Lord, you set your cross before us as a symbol of hope and love.
Give courage to all who are anxious or fearful in their sufferings . . .
May the weary be sustained by your word.

Lord, you hold your cross before us at the hour of our death.
Hear us as we remember with love all who have died . . .
Do not be ashamed of us when you come in your glory.

Year C

God of abiding mercy
We will rejoice in you.

Remember, O Lord,
not our many offences and weaknesses but your loving mercy,
which has endured from of old and through all ages . . .
Increase in us charity to search with you for all who stray,
that they may find their way back to rejoice in the peace you bring.

Remember, O Lord,
not our stiff necks and over-inflated pride, but our desire to serve you
    and be instruments of your dawning Kingdom.
Inspire with your compassion and longing all politicians and civic
    leaders . . .
Bring us all to rejoice in your freedom.

Remember, O Lord,
not our divisions and petty squabbles, but your desire to draw everyone
    into a community in which all can flourish . . .
May we rejoice together in the restoration you bring.

Remember, O Lord,
not our frustrated anger but your overwhelming compassion and pity . . .
In all, may we learn to trust and rejoice in your abiding love.

Remember, O Lord,
not our failures and everything we have left undone, but your unending
    mercy and love . . .
Bring us to rejoice in your eternal promise.

Proper 20
(Between 18 and 24 September)

Year A

Lord of faith and truth
We bless your holy name.

Generous God, you call all to work for your Kingdom.
Give your Church grace to rejoice when anyone joins in this ministry . . .
Striving side by side, we rejoice in your service.

Generous God, you challenge the limits of our employment terms with
    your justice.
Strengthen conditions of service that enhance our humanity . . .
Direct us to view one another as more than economic units.

Generous God, you are the giver of gifts and source of our talents.
Turn drudgery into a vehicle of your divine glory . . .
Transform our labours to reflect your creating presence.

Generous God, you bless us beyond the limitations of our physical
    condition.
Open our eyes to the mystery of your love in our human weakness . . .
Give us thankful hearts for your redeeming love.

Generous God, you hold before us wages beyond our deserving.
Grant your eternal gift to those released from their labours . . .
Give us faith to desire our ultimate home with you.

Year B

We call upon your name, O Lord
Incline your ear to our prayer.

Lord Jesus, you turn the honours of the world upside down.
Keep your Church from love of status and pride . . .
Give us a servant heart.

Lord Jesus, you challenge rulers to be mindful of all their people.
Keep the nations from cravings that lead to oppression and violence . . .
Give wisdom to all who lead.

Lord Jesus, you give children a special regard and dignity.
Keep their well-being and safety at the forefront of our minds and
    practices . . .
Give strength to all involved in safeguarding and protection; sustain them
    in their work.

Lord Jesus, you embrace the path of suffering.
Keep in your gaze all whose health is ailing . . .
Give peace and hope to all in need.

Lord Jesus, you hold before us the hope of salvation.
Keep in your love all who have died . . .
Give eternal life to all the faithful departed.

Year C

God of abiding mercy
We will rejoice in you.

Blessed Lord, from the rising of the sun to its setting, we will praise you
   and you alone.
Keep your Church in this single-minded devotion . . .
Sustain us with your presence.

Blessed Lord, hear our prayers for those in high position,
that the dignity of all may be upheld and honoured . . .
Guide all nations in the ways of peace with justice.

Blessed Lord, turn our hearts from love of wealth and obsession with its
   false security.
Set us free to trust in your bounty and to be satisfied with sufficient . . .
Fix our hearts where true and lasting treasures may be found.

Blessed Lord, in your love and mercy, save us from the anger and
   bitterness that destroys the soul.
Quieten the raging hearts of those in distress and bring peace to troubled
   minds . . .
Lift us from dust and ashes to hope in you.

Blessed Lord, you desire the salvation of all people.
We commend to you all who have died . . .
Bring us to rejoice in your courts with thanksgiving.

Proper 21
(Between 25 September and 1 October)

Year A

Lord of faith and truth
We bless your holy name.

Lord, your Kingdom reaches from the heavens embracing the whole of
creation.
You call your Church to assist with your harvest, schooling people in
your love . . .
Give us willing hearts, hands and voices with which to respond to your
summons.

Lord, you search the secret motives of those called to leadership,
and reveal hypocrisy and virtue alike . . .
Give us courage to scrutinize those who rule, and strengthen their
integrity.

Lord, you see more fully into our hearts and all that we can become.
We thank you for those who affirm and encourage our growth and
development . . .
Bring us to flourish in the warmth of your regard.

Lord, you know our needs and concerns before we ask.
Hear us as we bring before you all who are ill or in special need . . .
Bless them and bring them to rejoice in you.

Lord, there is no darkness that can extinguish your eternal light.
In this faith we entrust to you those who have died . . .
Raise us with them to your eternal Kingdom.

Year B

We call upon your name, O Lord
Incline your ear to our prayer.

Lord, you call your Church to be purified for your service.
Set our wills on your Kingdom alone . . .
Cease our trivial squabbles and focus your Church on proclaiming your
  glory.

Lord, you call the nations to be at peace with one another.
Unite them in the pursuit of the good of all . . .
May none prosper at the expense of others.

Lord, you call us to live justly.
Strengthen all who uphold order and bring to account any that cause
  harm . . .
Turn us from the evil we do and the good we do not do.

Lord, you call us to care for all who are sick.
Anoint them with your Holy Spirit . . .
Raise them up to sing your praises.

Lord, your call brings us home.
Draw to yourself all who have died . . .
Restore them in your life and love.

Year C

God of abiding mercy
We will rejoice in you.

God of Abraham and Sarah,
you hold all life in the palm of your hand and see the secret thoughts of
    our hearts.
Keep us from complacency and becoming haughty . . .
Set our hopes on your rich provision.

God of Lazarus,
you hear the cry of all who live in poverty and hunger.
We pray for those responsible for welfare provision and distributing from
    the common purse . . .
Bring justice and righteousness to reign.

God of rich and poor,
we pray for our community.
Strengthen the bonds that unite us and lead to cohesive living . . .
Anoint your people with your Holy Spirit.

God of hope,
hear our prayer for all who are pierced by pains and struggle with
    oppressions of the mind, body or spirit . . .
Bring us to believe that you do indeed keep your promises for ever.

God of eternal glory,
we remember with thanksgiving all who have passed from this life . . .
Rooted and grounded in your love,
bring us all to share in the life that really is life.

Proper 22
(Between 2 and 8 October)

———◆◆◆———

Year A

Praise the Lord for he is good
Sing to God with thanksgiving.

Lord of the vineyard, rooted and grafted in you, your Church bears fruit
to your glory.
Nourish and strengthen it for the task you purpose . . .
Tend the vine you have planted.

Lord of the vineyard, you expect nations to produce the wine of
justice.
Raise up leaders who will promote conditions in which all may
flourish . . .
Defend the poor and weak, the vulnerable and those easily overlooked.

Lord of the vineyard, you give all people the ability to choose between
right and wrong.
Guide us in all our moral dilemmas and the new challenges we face . . .
Keep us from evil intent and sliding into destructive ways.

Lord of the vineyard, you prepare wholesome fruit to refresh and revive
us.
Quench our thirst for wholeness and healing . . .
Restore us in your mercy and bring us to declare your glory.

Lord of the vineyard, you hold before us the cup of salvation.
Raise up all who have died . . .
Bring us to share in the new wine of your Kingdom.

Year B

Righteous Lord
We wait on your Word.

Lord, your welcome embraces young and old, rich and poor.
Give your Church this hospitable heart, that all may find a place at your
table . . .
May your compassionate challenge set our standards.

Lord, devious men sought to entrap your Son.
Protect leaders from those who would distort their words,
and your people from those who would lie and deceive . . .
May your name be exalted in all the earth.

Lord, you make men and women in your image and enable us to share
in your love together.
Bless all who are married and sustain them in living their vows . . .
As your love never lets us go, so may marriage be a source of delight
and rejoicing.

Lord, you catch us when we fall and restore us.
Hold tenderly all who have faced abuse or are injured by broken
relationships . . .
May your blessing rest upon us all today and always.

Lord, in life and in death we will praise you.
We remember with love and thanksgiving all who have died . . .
Gather to yourself all children of your Kingdom.

Year C

Gracious Lord
Let your people rejoice in you.

Lord, we come before you with faltering faith, with doubts and
anxieties.
Teach us to wait patiently on your presence . . .
Rekindle within us the gift of your grace.

Lord, our land can feel a strange place to proclaim your glory.
Teach us to sing the song of your mercies anew . . .
We rejoice in your great faithfulness.

Lord, the land produces of your bounty and sustains us with all we need.
Teach us to be responsible stewards of creation and to share of your
goodness . . .
As we are thankful so make us mindful of the needs of all.

Lord, hear our prayer for all who are weary and whose labours seem
thankless.
In all our sorrows, restore our trust in your providential care . . .
Pour upon us all your compassionate love.

Lord, hear our prayer for all whose lives feel desolate and lonely.
Deal tenderly with those whose hearts are torn apart by grief . . .
Gather to yourself in gentleness and peace all the departed.

Proper 23
(Between 9 and 15 October)

Year A

Praise the Lord for he is good
Sing to God with thanksgiving.

Heavenly Father, you embrace your creation in your Son as a
  bridegroom and bride.
Set us ablaze in this intimacy with passion and desire for your
  Kingdom . . .
Set before all your Church the banquet of your love.

Heavenly Father, you demand that all be invited and none shut out.
Hear our prayer for those excluded and on the margins of our
  society . . .
Remove the barriers that prevent any from realizing all that they could
  become.

Heavenly Father, bless all embarking on covenanted relationships of
  fidelity and mutual giving.
We pray for all that supports marriage and family life . . .
Bless us through love that is shared.

Heavenly Father, as your love reaches beyond the confines of our gaze,
do not forget those in distress or whose tears are hidden from our
  sight . . .
Bring to them your peace that goes beyond our understanding and
  surprises us with joy.

Heavenly Father, you set a table before us and invite us to share in your celestial banquet.
Grant us to share in this feast with all your faithful servants who have gone before us . . .
We will rejoice and praise your name.

Year B

Righteous Lord
We wait on your Word.

God of goodness, you inspire our hearts to reach beyond personal wealth.
Excite your Church with the treasure of your eternal presence . . .
Teach us to place our trust in your grace and mercy alone.

God of goodness, you puncture the flattery of our lips with the honesty of your truth.
Direct our gaze beyond personal aggrandizement to struggle with the issues of our day . . .
Give to all political leaders wisdom to serve those they represent.

God of goodness, you fill the earth with rich resources.
Give us grace to use these for the benefit of all and the relief of need . . .
Gladden the hearts of all your people.

God of goodness, your love sees our strength and weakness.
Look in mercy on all whose hearts are faint . . .
Strengthen and uphold them in their troubles.

God of goodness, all things are possible with you.
Raise in your love those who have died . . .
Grant us to join all your saints before your throne of grace.

Year C

Gracious Lord
Let your people rejoice in you.

Jesus, Master, have mercy on your people and hear us as we call out to
you.
Pour upon your Church the gift of faith that is hopeful and thankful . . .
Give us grace to celebrate devotion whatever guise or form it takes.

Jesus, Master, give to those who direct public policy vision to see
beyond those with the highest profile to include those on the
margins . . .
Give to all your children the blessing of peace.

Jesus, Master, you enable all people to be children of the same heavenly
Father.
Remove the divisions of our making, uniting us as fellow citizens of
your Kingdom . . .
May no one be disregarded as unclean or have their worth demeaned.

Jesus, Master, be with all whose illness separates them from contact with
others or isolates them through fear . . .
Bring healing and wholeness by your grace and favour.

Jesus, Master, you hold all souls in life.
We bring to you all who have died . . .
May we all obtain the salvation that is in you.

Proper 24
(Between 16 and 22 October)

———————

Year A

Praise the Lord for he is good
Sing to God with thanksgiving.

King of love, all things come from you and belong to you.
Take our lives and consecrate them in your service . . .
Keep your Church focused on our hope in you and your hold on your
  creation.

King of love, in your Christ's response to those seeking his entrapment
  he reminded them not to put you to the test.
Open our hearts to truth and justice . . .
We pray for all who call political leaders to account.

King of love, you provide for all that we need to sustain our life.
Give us faith to place our money completely at your service . . .
Make us wise stewards of this currency of action.

King of love, proclaim your release to all in the grip of debt and
  poverty.
Give consolation to the anxious and desperate . . .
Restore our true fortunes, O Lord.

King of love, the fullness of your glory is hidden from our sight.
Draw into the bright splendour of your presence all who have died . . .
You call us by name and we will rejoice with you for ever.

Year B

Righteous Lord
We wait on your Word.

Servant Lord, you became as one of us that we may be at one with
you.
Give to your Church the same humility that it may seek to raise up all
people as heirs of your grace . . .
In your service we will find true glory.

Servant Lord, you endured power struggles among your closest
followers.
Give to all political leaders wisdom to understand the true purpose of
government . . .
Take away all self-seeking and desire for honour.

Servant Lord, you saw the corrosive effects of status.
Give to all the peace that comes from knowing we are valuable in your
sight . . .
Set our restless hearts at ease in your love.

Servant Lord, by your bruises we are healed.
Give to the anguished the light of your presence . . .
Be with us, O Lord, in all our troubles.

Servant Lord, you are the source of our salvation.
Give to all who have died new life in your eternity . . .
Remember, O Lord, the work of your hands that we may be with you
for ever.

Year C

Gracious Lord
Let your people rejoice in you.

We lift our eyes, O Lord, to the quiet hills of your presence.
Preserve us from all evil and malicious intent . . .
Watch over us, O Lord.

We lift our eyes, O Lord, to your justice.
Guide all who sit in judgement or whose political office gives
  responsibility for our common life . . .
Watch over us, O Lord.

We lift our eyes, O Lord, to your holy scriptures.
May its words be sweet as honey to our taste,
and equip your Church for the work to which you call it . . .
Watch over us, O Lord.

We lift our eyes, O Lord, to all who cry out day and night,
all who wrestle in the night with faith and fear . . .
Watch over us, O Lord.

We lift our eyes, O Lord, with all whose labours are done.
We give thanks for those whose lives have inspired and whose memory
  fills us with praise . . .
May we all come to see you face to face.

Proper 25
(Between 23 and 29 October)

———•◆•———

Year A

Praise the Lord for he is good
Sing to God with thanksgiving.

Jesus, Messiah, before you we kneel in adoration and praise.
As we love you with our whole hearts, so give us grace to show that
    love towards our neighbours and ourselves . . .
Drive from your Church any vestige of hatred.

Jesus, Messiah, before you rulers and governments are humbled.
May those who rule not come to regard those without power as less
    than themselves . . .
Maintain the equity of all people.

Jesus, Messiah, your love leaves no one untouched, especially ourselves.
Strengthen all that restores us in your image . . .
Cherish the children for whom you gave so much.

Jesus, Messiah, your compassion overflows beyond any boundaries of our
    imagination.
Anoint with your healing grace any in distress . . .
Give them the comfort of your Holy Spirit.

Jesus, Messiah, your love extends to the cross and resurrection.
Bring under this hope all who have died . . .
Fulfil the promise of your Kingdom.

Year B

Righteous Lord
We wait on your Word.

Jesus, Son of David, have mercy on your Church.
Pour out your healing Spirit on our divisions . . .
Cure the spiritual blindness that prevents us perceiving and following
   your call.

Jesus, Son of David, have mercy on the nations.
Pour out your healing Spirit bringing peace with justice . . .
Open our eyes to see the consequences of environmental destruction and
   pollution.

Jesus, Son of David, have mercy on our financial institutions.
Pour out your healing Spirit on all who are materially rich yet
   emotionally poor . . .
Restore the balance to our balance sheets to take account of human
   costs.

Jesus, Son of David, have mercy on all who call out for relief in their
   suffering.
Pour out your healing Spirit upon them . . .
Bring relief to all in need.

Jesus, Son of David, have mercy on all at the hour of their death.
Pour out your life-restoring Spirit on the faithful departed . . .
By your intercession may we find true peace with the Father.

Year C

Gracious Lord
Let your people rejoice in you.

Lord, you know the secrets of our hearts and the honesty of our
    devotion.
Keep your Church open and accepting of all who call upon your
    name . . .
Bless and guide your pilgrim people.

Lord, you are the hope of all the earth.
Direct all nations in the ways of peace with justice . . .
In the dawn and at dusk we will sing for joy.

Lord, you are in the midst of us and call us by your name.
Give us cause to rejoice in your common wealth . . .
Bring us to live in harmony with one another.

Lord, you know our needs before we ask.
Be merciful with all who travel through the desolate valley . . .
In the dry places of our living may we all find fresh springs of living
    water.

Lord, your love embraces everything you have made.
We commit to you all who have died . . .
May we come to dwell with them in your eternal temple.

Bible Sunday
(Alternative for Last Sunday after Trinity)

Years A, B and C

Lord, your Word is a lantern to our feet
The light upon our path.

Word of Truth, you set your Church ablaze with the fire of your love.
Feed and inspire the lives of your servants to walk by this light . . .
Bless and guide translators and scholars of the scriptures, that we may live
a lively and godly faith.

Word of Justice, your command sets the oppressed free and calls rulers to
account.
Raise up prophets and counsellors of wisdom and insight . . .
Give courage to all who speak for the voiceless and proclaim your
liberation.

Word of Hope, you are the bedrock of existence and our ultimate goal.
Let your grace flow to nourish and sustain all people . . .
Gather into one body people of every race and language, that songs of
rejoicing may resound throughout the world.

Word of Comfort and Consolation, you restore what is diminished and
recover what has been lost.
Give solace to the weary and mend the broken . . .
Pour out your oil of healing on all our wounds and afflictions.

Bible Sunday

Word of Life, you turn the darkness of death into the dawn of new life.
Raise, we pray, all who have died . . .
Turn our sorrow into dancing and tears into laughter once more.

Dedication Sunday
(Alternative for First Sunday in October or Last Sunday after Trinity)

Years A, B and C

Truly the Lord is in this place
This is the gate of heaven.

Lord of the heavens and earth, you need no place made by human hands
 to dwell among us.
Rather, we make a shelter when we encounter your presence.
Sanctify this house of prayer as a gateway to you . . .
Before you we stand on holy ground.

Lord of glory, you give 'craftsman's art and music's measure' to delight
 our senses.
Inspire our praise and raise our gaze to see the imprint of your image in
 your creation . . .
In this holy space make a sanctuary for your justice.

Lord of yesterday, today and the future,
you give to us a heritage of faith proclaimed in stone.
Build and restore your temples as living stones . . .
Give us wisdom to treasure and value what has been handed on without
 stifling your Spirit.

Lord of peace, you give to us space to be still and know that you are
 God.
Bring into our anxious concerns trust in your providential care . . .
Breathe upon us your life-restoring presence.

Lord of the harvest, you hold all life from beginning to its end, and
onwards to new life.

Bear as on eagles' wings your faithful servants who have departed this
life . . .

In union with the great cloud of witnesses who have worshipped in this
place, bring us all to rejoice in your heavenly home.

4 before Advent

———◆———

Year A

God our strength
We put our trust in you.

Lord, your Church faces many trials and conflicts.
Keep its eyes and heart on the gift of yourself in your Son . . .
Send us out to proclaim your Kingdom throughout the world.

Lord, nations rise against nations in war and hostile acts.
Give courage to those who dare to pursue peace . . .
Bring harmony and concord to all people.

Lord, many are hungry and homeless through famine and natural
    disasters.
Bless and guide the work of relief agencies and all who bring aid . . .
Bring us to our senses to end the over-consumption and squandering of
    the earth's resources that exacerbate environmental change.

Lord, the created order brings health and illness.
Hold us through moments of strength and weakness . . .
In all our joys and sorrows we give you thanks and praise.

Lord, you bring life and death and in your mercy new life.
Raise, we pray, all the departed . . .
Comfort all who mourn with the good news of your saving love.

Year B

Give thanks to the Lord with your whole heart
Call upon his name.

Lord, you set your commandments on the foundation of love.
Inspire your Church to display this devotion in thought, word and
deed . . .
Give us grace to walk in your ways.

Lord, help us to build our nation on the foundation of your truth.
Inspire men and women rooted in your wisdom to engage with
politics . . .
Give to everyone of goodwill a willingness to work for the benefit of all.

Lord, do not leave yourself without witnesses and people called after
your name.
Inspire those who teach, that the gospel may capture the imaginations of
the young . . .
Give enthusiasm for living the way of your Son.

Lord, you require us to extend our concern to all in need.
Inspire all who work to relieve suffering and care for the sick . . .
Give them hope in your enduring love.

Lord, by your blood you obtain our eternal redemption.
Inspire our hearts to trust in your salvation . . .
Give life everlasting to your faithful departed.

Year C

God of mercy
Speak your words of peace.

Lord, you stand in judgement over the emptiness of our praise.
In your mercy make us worthy of our calling . . .
Fulfil by your power every good resolve and glorify your name.

Lord, you stand in judgement over the rulers of this age.
Turn the grumbles of the proud to the gratitude of the penitent . . .
Bring your salvation to our house today.

Lord, you stand in judgement over relationships that diminish and bring
    dishonour.
Strengthen all that enables us to flourish and grow in your grace . . .
Reclaim us, Lord, as your sons and daughters.

Lord, you bring healing and release to all held captive by the bonds of
    guilt and despising eyes.
Deliver your people in whatever their anguish or distress . . .
Preserve us, O Lord, and surround us with your deliverance.

Lord, you came to seek out and to save the lost.
Look in mercy on all who have died . . .
Bring us to share in the eternal banquet of your love.

All Saints Sunday
(Between 30 October and 5 November)

———◆◆◆———

Year A

Sing to the Lord a new song
Let the faithful rejoice.

Blessed Lord, your Son turned expectations upside down by offering the
   Kingdom to the poor and persecuted.
Give your Church faith to trust in you and not in riches or trappings of
   power . . .
Strengthen all who suffer for following you.

Blessed Lord, you called peacemakers your children and honoured those
   who hunger and thirst for righteousness.
Bring in your justice and equity . . .
Guide all in political office to walk in your mercy and truth.

Blessed Lord, you show yourself to the pure in heart.
Give us contrite hearts for all that blurs our vision of you . . .
Forgive us the sins that separate us from one another and from you.

Blessed Lord, we will bless you at all times.
Give us voice to praise you in darkness and light . . .
Revive us, O Lord, and make us whole.

Blessed Lord, you comfort all who mourn and give cause for rejoicing.
Be with all whose hearts ache with grief . . .
Salvation belongs to you and you wipe every tear from our eyes.

Year B

Sing to the Lord a new song
Let the faithful rejoice.

Lord of life, you delight your people with a vision of your celestial city.
Inspire your Church by the lives of your saints . . .
Make us holy as you are holy.

Lord of life, you raise our expectations and challenge us to match them.
Inspire leaders to reach beyond the limits of convention and the status
quo . . .
Make us joyful as you are joyful.

Lord of life, you spread before us a banquet of your love.
Inspire us to share the fruits of your bounty . . .
Make us gracious as you are gracious.

Lord of life, you bring an end to pain and suffering.
Inspire us to work for the relief of need and the comfort of distress . . .
Make us compassionate as you are compassionate.

Lord of life, you wipe away tears, and death will be no more.
Inspire us to long for your eternity . . .
Make us live as you live and reign in glory.

Year C

Sing to the Lord a new song
Let the faithful rejoice.

Blessed Lord, you bring all things to fulfilment in your Son.
Set our hope always on Christ that we may live to your praise and
  glory . . .
With heart and voice we sing of your wonder and splendour.

Blessed Lord, you turn the fortunes of the poor and hungry,
and of the self-satisfied and those who seek easy praises.
Shine your light on our common living . . .
Bring all nations to rejoice in their maker.

Blessed Lord, your Holy Spirit transforms our conflicts so that the paths
  of peace and reconciliation may be opened . . .
May all your children have cause to be joyful.

Blessed Lord, you hear the cries of all in pain and misery.
We bring before you those in any kind of distress . . .
Mark us all with the seal of your promised Spirit.

Blessed Lord, in Christ we have a heritage that is unfading.
In this hope we remember your saints throughout the ages . . .
May all your holy ones be received into the Kingdom without end.

3 before Advent

Year A

We will rejoice and be glad in you
We will trust in your mercy.

Lord Jesus, as a bridegroom you invite us to celebrate the wedding
banquet of your love for the whole world.
Keep your Church ready and willing to welcome you in heart, mind
and deed . . .
Give us grace to shine as lights to your glory.

Lord Jesus, you call us to live in readiness for your Kingdom.
Give to all who take counsel for the nations wisdom to look beyond the
immediate and to prioritize by the values of your eternity . . .
May your righteousness flow like a river.

Lord Jesus, in your generous mercy you make strangers friends and unite
all people in a commonwealth.
Forgive our warring madness and the violence that is so often
employed . . .
Let your peace and justice flourish.

Lord Jesus, we bring before you all injured, maimed and scarred by
warfare and aggression . . .
Bind up our wounds and send forth your healing Spirit.

Lord Jesus, you hold all souls in life and regard no one with contempt.
Bring into your Kingdom all who have died . . .
At the last trumpet call raise us to your eternity.

Year B

We wait on you, O Lord
Our hope is in your mercy.

Lord Jesus Christ, you called brothers to leave their boats at the lakeside
and follow you.
Give your Church courage to step out in new ways to proclaim your
good news . . .
May we trust in the power of your gospel.

Lord Jesus Christ, your call confronts us with the need for repentance.
Turn the hearts of all to the values of your Kingdom . . .
Forgive our conflicts and destructive ways.

Lord Jesus Christ, you drew working men into your company.
Guide all responsible for industrial relations and fair conditions of
work . . .
Expand concern for price to embrace the costs borne by everyone.

Lord Jesus Christ, you came among human life and shared in its joys and
sorrows.
Bless all who are struggling with the strains of care . . .
May the sound of your call refresh us.

Lord Jesus Christ, your nets encompass all humanity.
Gather to yourself all who have died . . .
Bring us to rejoice in your saving love.

Year C

We call upon you, O God
Incline your ear to our prayer.

Holy God, you sanctify your people through the power of your Holy
  Spirit.
Keep us firm in the faith and united in truth . . .
Strengthen your Church in the hope of Christ.

Holy God, we lift your name on high and exalt you above all others.
Keep those in authority from the paths of destruction and vanity . . .
May peace and justice flourish.

Holy God, your love draws us closer into your presence.
Bless our homes and relationships, those we love and who love us . . .
Open our hearts to embrace friend and stranger.

Holy God, be with all whose footsteps stumble
and who cry out to you in their frailty . . .
Keep and protect them under your loving gaze.

Holy God, as we know our redeemer lives,
hear our prayer for all who have died . . .
Grant us at the last to see you face to face.

2 before Advent

———◆◆◆———

Year A

We will rejoice and be glad in you
We will trust in your mercy.

Generous God, you share of yourself in diverse gifts.
Help us to use what we are given to grow your Kingdom . . .
Keep your Church from concern only for itself and the fear that
    paralyses action.

Generous God, your bountiful love blesses the earth.
Inspire wise and fair stewardship of these riches . . .
Turn our hearts from greed and abuse of your creation.

Generous God, you set us as a body with many limbs and organs.
Combine these different callings and abilities into a wonderful symphony
    of your transforming love . . .
United in you we will sing your praises.

Generous God, we give you thanks for the skill and talent of medical
    practitioners.
In your mercy be with those who call upon you in their frailty . . .
Pour out your healing blessing and mercy.

Generous God, you give life and give it abundantly.
Raise all our dearly departed brothers and sisters to your salvation . . .
We will rejoice in the joy of your Kingdom.

Year B

We wait on you, O Lord
Our hope is in your mercy.

God of truth, your Son warned against false devotion.
Keep your Church from being led astray by deviations and perversions of
  your truth . . .
May we never confuse your house of prayer with your eternal presence.

God of truth, your Son warned of wars and rumours of wars.
Keep the nations from the paths of death and destruction . . .
Forgive our warring madness which scars the face of the earth and its
  people.

God of truth, your Son warned of earthquakes and famines.
Keep us from making disasters worse by failures of compassion . . .
Bless the work of relief agencies.

God of truth, your Son warned of calamities to come.
Keep us from despair in our frailty . . .
Deliver us in our hour of need.

God of truth, your Son promised to rebuild the temple of his body.
Restore to life all who have died . . .
Bring us to share with you in your Kingdom.

Year C

Shout with joy to the Lord
We lift our voices to rejoice in you.

Bountiful Lord, we lift our voices to rejoice and sing of your praises.
Hear our prayer for all who testify to your name in the face of
persecution and threats of violence . . .
Keep your Church from alarm that sends it astray.

Bountiful Lord, forgive the sins that set nation against nation, brothers
and sisters against their family and displace people to famine and
disease . . .
With righteousness and equity bring your peace to reign.

Bountiful Lord, you bless us with gifts of music.
Teach us to sing a new song of salvation and hope in your Son . . .
May the river of your life flow to refresh the land.

Bountiful Lord, your compassion touches all who suffer from disease and
natural disasters.
Hear our prayer for all whom we carry on our hearts into your
presence . . .
Sun of righteousness, bring your healing touch to all who call upon your
name.

Bountiful Lord, you hold all souls in life.
We give you thanks for those whose faith has endured through many
trials and tribulations . . .
Give rest to your faithful ones, that they may rise in your glory.

Christis the King

-------◆◆◆-------

Year A

Give thanks to the Lord
Exalt his holy name.

Christ our King, your justice embraces all people and calls us into a
  mutual fellowship of love and care.
Challenge your Church to live out this concern in acts of compassion
  and liberation . . .
As we do to and for others, so we serve you.

Christ our King, give to governments and all who rule a deep concern
  for the needs of their people.
Give us an openness to welcome the stranger in peace and hospitality . . .
May we share of our wealth and poverty.

Christ our King, in you the thirsty find refreshment, the hungry are fed,
  the naked are clothed and prisoners are visited.
Leave no one ignored and abandoned . . .
Extend the boundaries of our concern beyond those who are easy to
  love.

Christ our King, the sick, the lame and the infirm hold a special place in
  your concern.
Give us grace to ensure that the care that is needed is provided . . .
As your faithfulness endures from age to age, so we rejoice before your
  glory.

Christ our King, you wept at the tomb of Lazarus and restored a little
    girl to life.
Bring all the faithful departed to eternity with you . . .
Gather to yourself all the blessed of your Father.

Year B

The Lord is king
Let the people rejoice.

Lord Jesus Christ, your Kingdom encompasses the whole world and
    stretches beyond the heavens.
Renew your Church to trust in your providence and victory . . .
Strengthen the faint-hearted in the face of persecution and turmoil.

Lord Jesus Christ, you stood before Pilate with dignity and integrity.
Give wisdom and discernment to all who govern,
that truth may be heard and honoured . . .
By your grace, may peace prevail.

Lord Jesus Christ, at your arrest many deserted you and a few watched
    from the shadows.
Be with those who face trial alone and with appropriate adults who
    accompany accused juveniles . . .
By your redeeming power, give us opportunity to amend our ways.

Lord Jesus Christ, you chose to subject yourself to human frailty.
By your presence, bless us in our weakness . . .
Hold us in your love.

Lord Jesus Christ, you embraced death and made it the gateway to glory.
Do not forsake us at the hour of our death . . .
Bring us to rejoice in your eternal Kingdom.

Year C

Rejoice in the Lord
Sing to him with thanksgiving.

Christ our King, enthroned on the cross bearing insults and torments for
our redemption, by your blood may true peace reign . . .
Bless and guide your body, the Church, that we may exalt you and share
in the inheritance of the saints in light.

Christ our King, you endured the scoffing of leaders and ridicule from
bystanders.
Rescue us from the grip of darkness and cynical abuses of power . . .
Strengthen all who strive for justice by your glorious power.

Christ our King, still our hearts to know your presence and share your
peace . . .
Bring us to declare that you are our righteousness.

Christ our King, in lonely agony you bore the pains of the world.
Be with all who are desolate and afflicted, whose world is shaken . . .
Be a present help, O Lord, in times of trouble and give courage and
strength to all who fear.

Christ our King, gather in your mercy all who have shared in your
passion, whose earthly striving has ceased . . .
May we with them come to be with you in paradise.